The Poeming Pigeon
A Journal of Poetry & Prose

The Poeming Pigeon
A Journal of Poetry & Prose

Volume 2, Issue 1
Doobie or Not Doobie?

A Publication of The Poetry Box®

©2016 The Poetry Box®
All rights reserved.
Each poem/story copyright reserved by individual authors.
Original Cover Illustration & Photographs by Robert R. Sanders.
Editing & Book Design by Shawn Aveningo Sanders.
Cover Design by Robert R. Sanders.
Printed in the United States of America.

No part of this book may be reproduced
in any matter whatsoever without written
permission from the author, except in the case
of brief quotations embodied in critical essays,
reviews and articles.

Library of Congress Control Number: 2016932773

ISBN-13: 978-0-9863304-8-3
ISBN-10: 0986330485

Published by The Poetry Box®, 2016
Beaverton, Oregon
www.ThePoetryBox.com
530.409.0721

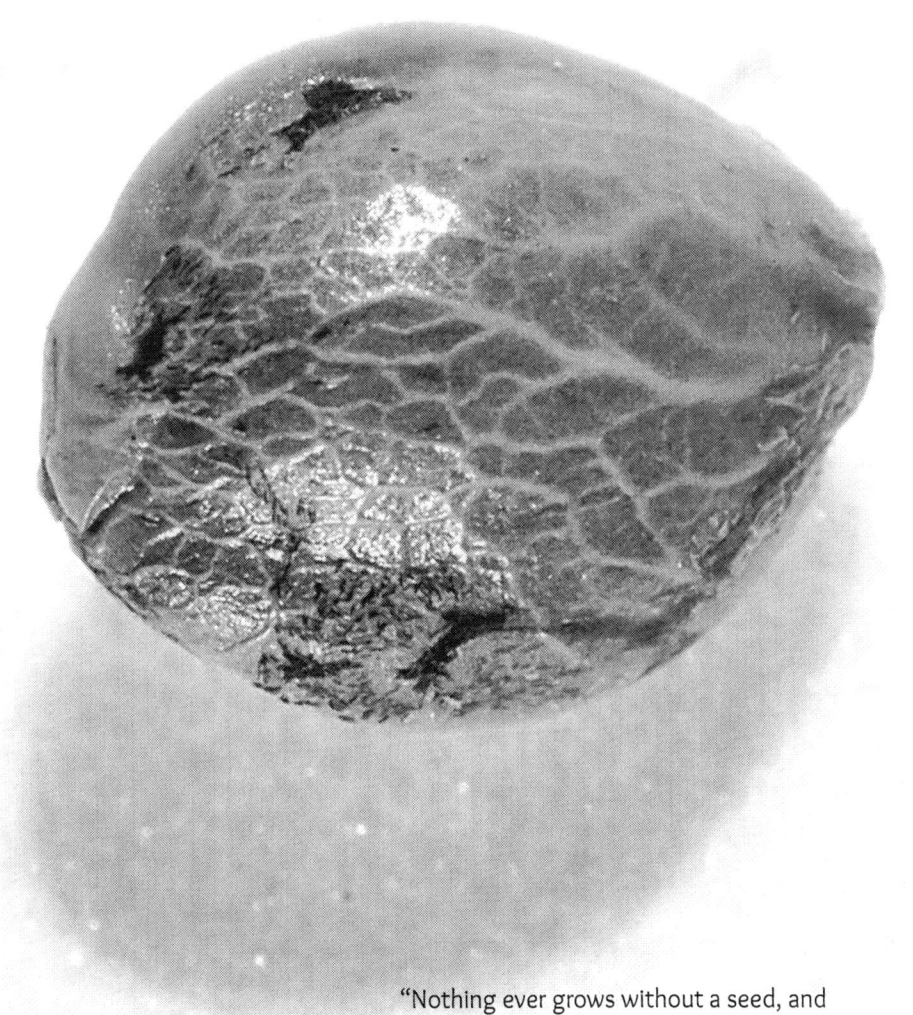

"Nothing ever grows without a seed, and nothing ever changes without a dream."
~ Debby Boone

Contents

Introduction 11
High-ku ~*Angi Holden* 15
Maria Juana ~*Paco Marquez* 16
Crick ~*Jake Grieco* 17
Sinsemilla ~*Sigrun Susan Lane* 18
In the Swamp of '96 ~*Phoebe Levija* 19
No, It's Called Flower ~*Judith Skillman* 21
Flowers ~*S.K. Kelen* 22
Seeds and Stems ~*Michael Berton* 25
Renewable Resource ~*SM* 27
Study Confirms: Smells Trigger Memories ~*Lori Loranger* 28
Vanilla Zeppelin ~*Catfish McDaris* 29
Festival ~*Eric Silvera* 30
Gravity ~*Karen Jane Cannon* 32
Smoking Babbs' Weed ~*Doug Draime* 33
Exaggerating the Present ~*Tim Kahl* 34
Stay Present ~*Kerry A. Bennett* 35
The Lost Years ~*Jayne Martin* 36
I Did Not Inhale ~*Jane James* 38
Mary, Mary, Not Contrary ~*Jim Fulcomer* 39
The Farmer of Leeds 2.0 ~*Wayne Lee* 40
So Poor ~*Carl "Papa" Palmer* 41
The Wrong Indians ~*Peter D. Goodwin* 42
Cadence of the Latest Century ~*William Doreski* 44
It's ... um ... 4:20 ~*Karen Robiscoe* 47
Oh, the Places You'll Purchase It ~*Brandyn Johnson* 48
Edward Albee Knew the Score ~*Christopher Luna* 50
Green ~*Jennifer Pratt-Walter* 51
Exhaling Drags ~*Adrian Ernesto Cepeda* 52

The Pothead Lover ~Carolyn Smuts 53
My Marriage to Merry-Jane ~Tricia Knoll 54
Tarot Readings ~Rebecca Bilkau 55
Tea Leaf and Cannabis Reader ~Eileen Malone 57
In the Air ~Jade Ware 59
Passive Smoking ~Angi Holden 60
When I Was Your Age ... ~Katy Brown 61
First and Last ~Brad G. Garber 62
Crazy Enough ~Katy Brown 65
Have You? ~LOB 66
In 1967, Mom Never Bought Paper Towels ~Spurs Broken 68
The First Time ~Leona Phillips 70
Toucans & Reindeer ~Chella Courington 71
Tokus ~Cathy Bryant 72
At First, It Was a Sleep Aid ~Lydia Flores 73
Dream Panther ~Pattie Palmer-Baker 76
In the Campground ~Karla Linn Merrifield 77
I Smoked a Spider ~Casey Bush 78
The Erratic Train ~Nathan Tompkins 80
Trippin' ~John Smistad 82
Personal History ~Bill Gainer 86
David Lerner: One for the Holidaze ~David Belmont 87
In Reference to Shakespeare's Sonnet 76 and Recent News
  ~D. Russel Micnhimer 90
Reaching Back with Each Drag ~Adrian Ernesto Cepeda 91
I've Walked Down ~Alec Solomita 92
Temporal Pastoral ~Devin Taylor 93
Fractured ~Rachael Clyne 94
Saturday Night, Upcountry Maui ~Burky Achilles 96
Lovesong ~Halee Kirkwood 98
Ne – Neon 10 ~Marj Hahne 99

Free 99 ~*Jake Grieco* 100

Smoke Screens ~*Teresa Zemaitis* 102

The Pipe, the Plants, and the Misdemeanor ~*Sarah White* 105

Stolen Dances ~*Jill Hawkins* 106

Smoked Out ~*Helen Sparrow* 107

After the Law Changed ~*Marilyn Stablein* 109

Northwest Soma ~*Leah Mueller* 110

Ivy and Weed ~*Shawn Aveningo* 112

Lefty ~*John Lambremont, Sr.* 114

Barack'O's Toback'O ~*Karen Robinscoe* 116

CannaBaloney ~*Art Goodtimes* 118

Lost to Regulation ~*Judith Skillman* 119

Herbal Emancipation ~*Jade Ware* 120

The Wrapped Lace ~*Richard Bannerman* 121

Medicine Smoke ~*Kerry A. Bennett* 123

Dirty Girl ~*Kristin Roedell* 125

We're Goin' to Sev (c. 1995) ~*Christopher Luna* 127

A Joint Circle ~*Nathan Tompkins* 128

New York High ~*Tiffany Burba-Schramm* 129

Getting High ~*Tiffany Burba-Schramm* 130

Priming the Pump for a Fire ~*Scott Thomas Outlar* 131

The Devil's Lettuce ~*Tim Kahl* 132

Erev Rosh Hashanah 5773 ~*Barbara Ruth* 133

When You Run Out of Papers, There's Always the Gideon
 ~*Mercedes Webb-Pullman* 134

Living Easy ~*Bill Gainer* 135

High Above the Pain ~*Doug Draime* 136

Acknowledgments 139

Contributors 141

Index of Authors (by last name) 151

About The Poetry Box® 153

Introduction

For the times they are a-changin'.
~ Bob Dylan

When Robert and I first came up with the idea for this book, I couldn't help but flashback to my 8th grade Health Class where Mr. Grimes, stood in front of the blackboard, with white chalk smears on his navy trousers, and warned us of the dangers of marijuana use. As he revealed the classic "This is your brain; this is your brain on drugs" poster, Tim Crannell turned around in the desk in front of me and offered me a joint! I was terrified of getting sent directly to the principal's office and having the 'wacky-weed' noted on my 'permanent record.' So yes, the times are indeed changing, as has my attitude toward the herb, now almost four decades later.

Marijuana, it seems, has infused itself in my life in a myriad of ways. And in reading the submissions of poems and stories that arrived in my inbox from all over the world, I have come to realize there is so much to learn (and un-learn) about this miracle plant. Even what we call it has now changed to a more socially acceptable vernacular, as demonstrated in Judith Skillman's poem, "*No, It's Called Flower:*"

> *Weed is seen in a bad light,*
> *he explained, for its connotations ...*
> *... flower is pretty, more acceptable.*

But alas, no matter how we dress it up, a rose by any other name would still smell as skunky, to most. The legalization and regulation of cannabis in our country, and others across the globe, has become a hot topic for heated debate. It's an issue that isn't necessarily clearly cut down political party lines. But alas, the desire for legalization is one that's more openly supported by those on the left, as John Lambremont, Sr. illustrates in his tale about a lab mouse named "Lefty:"

> ... instead preferring the cannabinoid
> and the mellow blow he so enjoyed.
> They all called him Lefty ...
> he was perpetually hungry

Medical marijuana has been a bipartisan issue in many states such as Florida, for several years. Close-call ballot measures narrowly defeated have summoned calls-to-action for some governors to sign various versions of a Compassionate Medical Cannabis Act, allowing limited use to alleviate pain for cancer patients, Lou Gehrig's disease, or epilepsy.

Meanwhile, many continue the fight to decriminalize the drug and remove its 'Schedule 1' status to open the doors for further research into the possible healing and curing properties of cannabis. Until then, many patients are often forced to make the difficult choice between getting addicted to prescribed opiates or breaking local law to relieve their suffering. And some are lucky to find compassion in unexpected places, like Megan found in Teresa Zemaitis' story, "Smoke Screens:"

> [the nurse] whispered, "if you get some, I'll prop open
> the side door for you. But if you get caught, you're on
> your own."

Regardless of what side of the debate you land, its important to be part of the conversation. It's imperative that as responsible adults we seek out knowledge and investigate to separate fact from propaganda. An individual may not possess the desire to dab, vape, smoke or ingest cannabis-infused treats, but perhaps it's more about freedom of choice. Helen Sparrow's story, "Smoked Out," has a fun surprise ending that speaks to this very idea. As does Tim Kahl's poem "The Devil's Lettuce:"

> Yes, I'm sure our sheer joy is highly taxable,
> and this pure euphoria is just a rental,

> but who am I to tell you how you should own
> the time you spend in a chair.

In reading this book, you'll find a variety of voices, albeit most seem to favor the doobie side of the *Doobie or Not Doobie* question. And for many, it's merely a fun look into the rear-view mirror of coming of age, filled with tales of music, mayhem, munchies and Mary-Jane.

So kick back ... Light up (or don't) ... And most of all, enjoy the ride!

~ Shawn Aveningo
March, 2016

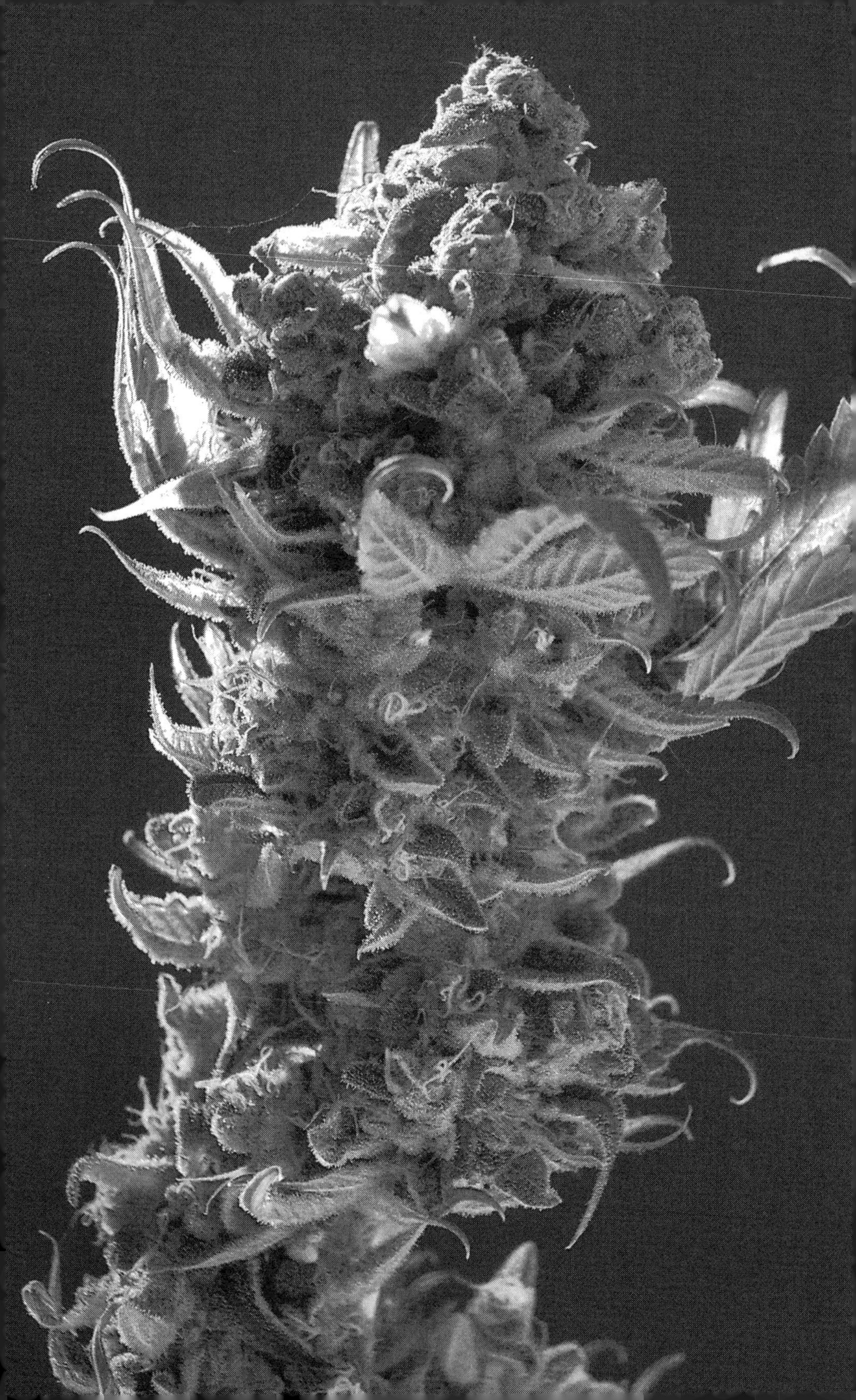

Angi Holden

High-ku

This leaf opens out

like a hand, an offering:

a cool breath of peace.

Paco Marquez

Maria Juana

Green memory Menthol soul
Sacred fluorescent emerald
Wild soil chemistry
Fiery crisscross hairy ball
Mountain scent of pine tree's heart

Moist, dark-green moss
with intricate, minute, stem patterns—
like old rope knots

Brake a piece as sweet bread
to melt the mouth with milk
Watch the fireball
crunching, sizzling

Rosicross Alacross
Rosicross Alacross

Forbidden
hidden
blue-cross vineyards
Abyss leading to a rainbow cellar

Crick

what you don't know is I don't know
where we're going
I only know I want orange juice
candy & ecstasy & a subway

                                              & a painting of the goddess
                                                       your nipples, you model
                                                      your body a watercolor
                                                        creek full of crawdads

they are little lobster creatures
I say & you laugh like Mary

                                              those thirty years Jesus was
                                                              missing

he was eating pizza &
watching anime & we all love
Australian Shepard's

                       our thumbs wrestle
                       our feet shuffle
                       up the mountain

                                          we forgot our crosses but
                                    we have plenty of water & weed
                                      to feed each other lifetimes

Sigrun Susan Lane

Sinsemilla
~ For Mike

She stands taller than my brother
the gardener, cut down
by the cancer that has quieted him.
Slim and graceful, she flaunts jungle
green leaves in Snohomish sun.

She yearns for a mate.
The air is scented with her desire.
In her stalk the thick flow of juices,
her clumped yellow flowers are sticky with resin.
We stand in her narrow shade
breathe in the sun, her essence.

She is both *Sativa* and *Indica*—
baked in a brownie, her buds
carry goodness for mind and body.
From the hot equator *Sativa* brings
bursts of euphoria, a hilarious elephant
ride in Rangoon, laughter like champagne.

From the Hindu Kush, the body's bliss—
an evening float on the upper Ganges
in gentle calm under falling stars.
But she flowers near the Stillaguamish,
you can almost hear the dirt hum,
in the planted rows of the patient gardener.

Phoebe Levija

In the Swamp of '96

Daddy needs to trim.
He leads me to the greenhouse

behind our rotting trailer,
deep in sovereign backwoods.

We walk through trails of
wilting rocks and cypress spires

as pine needles lay corpse
pose beneath our feet.

The silver of swamp lilies
lip the land in pale haze

and a veil of Spanish moss tickles
my nose like gauzey ginger ale.

Daddy's greenhouse is a shed,
a haven. A milieu of magic

and fleur-de-cannabis.
Pixies pull my plaits

while gnomes dance
under mushroom parasols.

Daddy dips his hands
into the loam, befriending

muddy earthworms. He says
he feels akin to the natural world,

the yellow blood of a butterfly
and pale jade of perplexing geckos.

Daddy is a shaman. He trims
holy blooms that come from

spirits who sing in the wind
like the whippoorwill at dusk.

Snipping sticky bushels, Daddy
packs his pipe, carved in the shape

of a sullen armadillo.
I watch him inhale.

His breath
      stiff

    as a braid of mangroves

   he exhales a ligneous cough

  I don't mind,
      much.

No, It's Called Flower

Not weed, I was told
by the young man
behind the counter.
Weed is seen in a bad light,
he explained, *for its connotations.*

Flower—here he gestured
at thick buds of Kush,
Strawberry Pie, and Diesel
filling glass jars,
spilling their scent

into the room, arrayed
in shades of verdant green,
huge buds horny as hell
for what they'd been deprived of.
—*Flower is pretty, more acceptable.*

I applaud your rebranding,
I said, the question
of how to inhale
without burning my throat
still there on my lips, unasked.

S. K. Kelen

Flowers

Happy combustions bring a restless calm,
The Thesaurus falls open at an obscure word.
Yandi a Koori noun meaning a hidden place
Where a herb is kept from the rest of the world.
A blessing or a cursed stimulant, it gets you
One way or another yet always
Works as a sacrament. Weird yoga—
Inhale smoke deeply and words walk backwards
In the mind, circumnavigate and run away
Leaving the pleasure of dilemmas.
The body and mind find harmony
Vague and dreamy, the music of the spheres
Is all fuzzy at the edges.
The wacky thesaurus's pages crumble
Words melt, find their way into a pipe
A match strikes, smoke rises fills rooms with Peace
The kind of peace bright thoughts pervade.
A hot day at the Bong-Bong races
Smoke pours out the horses' ears
As they snort around the track
Jockeys ripped to the eyeballs
Or when on a dusty plain
In central India the wind puffs bhang
From a hookah the sadhu cries *bom-shenka!*
How ancient buddha reminds us to be up to date
Old fashioned, punctual and always late.
Take the heat and hardship crumbling mulled heads
Weed, wacky tobacky, dakka akkity
Time outdoors is time you could
Be at home getting stoned
With a healthy deal, splendid hashish
Blended with golden pineapple
Paw-paw and mango juice

Plenty of spit goes into hashish
Congealing its numb pollen dumbness
Flame of the East, or a skunky lover
Heading, budding, light and crash
There's a hybrid for every geography
Northern and southern. Tijuana Gold
Moroccan Pale or Lebanese Blonde,
Paki Black and Nimbin Red
Mullumbimby Madness, good old Queensland Heads
Durban Poison and Blackman's Bush
Hooch and chuff, they all do the trick,
the mountains of Nepal bloom sex on a stick.
Searched by a border guard—have a smoke
With her and her lips are as sweet as the taste
Of the maiden Sinsemilla.
A jar in Tennessee was filled with resinous buds.
Huffing and puffing flowery pot
Grown under the sun's hippy eyelid
From forest deep or indoors under angel lights
Fragrant hydroponic—life in a submarine—
The bad health bubbles up
Music that soothes the savage soul
And the addled wolf will never find the door—
A stereo steadies heart
Spooked to the power of many
All the fun of the fair, with vigour of Mind
Move a cloud for a while
Dark sometimes don't care
Knowing all the time it's wrong
But as vices go it's not so bad
It's kind of noble
Stoking, smoking, choking
Eyes exploding
A chillum for your thoughts
Ma'am? or just the mist lifting
Falling, crazy astral travelling—
Compadre we are lost

Stunned joy eating—
All over town, grasshoppers fly.
Frogs croak and trees advise.
Feeling creative?
Transport to a dark pleasure dome—
There's a light! A light!
Good ganja saves.
The mind mulls over it, hmmm
Doomed to an eternal passing phase
Walk, don't drive. It's so stupid—
What's great is great dope.
Abundant happiness—the lungs
And throat protest too much—
Practise right breathing
To increase inspiration powers
Always edgy, paranoid and desperate with hope
Time stands still yet the hours rush
You're walking there among the wholesome flowers.
Yet even a reggae life must pass
Quiet days valley to valley
And flowers of grass.

Michael Berton

Seeds and Stems

in the days of seeds and stems
when 8-tracks hissed and squeaked
your youth into a blur of riff solos
everybody played Hendrix air guitar
while acquiring cottonmouth munchies
on a Cheech and Chong double date

the stoners & freaks had etiquette
dropping names like
Kona Gold
Acapulco Primo
Oaxacan Red Bud
Maui Wowie
and attitudes that they
goofed you into thinking
they were straight

somebody's black-sheep uncle
flew it all across the border
planes loaded levitated
landing in the desert
with illicit contraband
running for cover in sandstorms
as the DEA patrolled the skies
and local yokels the streets
where paranoia annoyance
crept behind the wheel
under the dash
of hotrods and lowriders
fueled by machismo
marking infraction on the scene

in classrooms studious
students at their desks reading
the latest High Times issue
hidden behind textbooks
the class clown
up at the pencil sharpener
practicing finger prowess
by using pencil shavings
to blimp up zig zag papers
it was NORML
calling for decriminalization
while we methodically
separated the seeds and stems
out from the sweat leaf
then we partied
at the Hotel California
with The Band On The Run
and the Excitable Boy
with Sticky Fingers
from Houses of The Holy
full of Toys In The Attic

later in lotus position
hypnotized by mood lamps
bong gurgling on a lid
time/spacing on the
dark side with Pink
where we could isolate
an instrument
from the song and
ride out its sound
in stoner time
a parallel dimension
to real time
in make-believe scenarios
that went down as
cannabis brainstorming

S.M.

Renewable Resource

When legalized—there will be books:
    Marijauna for Dummies
    Mary Jane for You and Me
    Pull Your Own Weed
How to plant, pinch, harvest, seed.
There will be instruction books on how to roll,
how to inhale, blow smoke rings,
meet the munchies on your own terms,
how to look cool when you're too stoned
to know yourself in a mirror.
There will be books, recipes
    for pot brownies
    hashish hashbrowns
    merry marimary's little lamb
Who knows? There may even be TV shows:
    Gardening with Cannabis Bob
    Painting from Seed
    The Dancing Doobies
Bedtime stories told to children:
    The Three Pot-bellied Pigs
    The Little Doobie That Could ...
    Sticks and Stoners May Break my Bones
    Single-minded and Double Jointed
Books on statistics, medical reports
Lung cancer this, lung cancer that
Too stoned to notice pain, too stoned to care
Of course, these books will be made of hemp,
recyclable, and of paper ready to roll.

Lori Loranger

Study Confirms: Smells Trigger Memories

Soothing aroma
memorized in kegger basements
decades ago
masking scents of sweat and beer;
peace pipe calmness overpowering even alcohol-fueled
beer brawling rage

"Relax Man, it's cool – I've got some ass kickin' Colombian"
Circle forms, lighter flaring at the center,
like Neanderthals around a fire,
evolving into more sapient hominids amid the coughing haze
of what must be laughing gas,
'cause pretty soon everything's funny, especially
whatever they were fighting about.

Thick sticky clouds of eye-watering hilarity
sweetly morphing common thoughts into dancing daydreams,
bruised egos into brotherly love

That mirth making scent
starts Led Zeppelin and Pink Floyd singing in my head
makes me remember how to play drunk backgammon
reminds me why I don't drink much beer anymore.
Over these 40 years I've learned more beer does not equal more fun,
but that sweet smoky smell
still brings me peace.

Catfish McDaris

Vanilla Zeppelin

Combed Yale Park on Route 66
For psychedelics, scored orange sunshine & chocolate mescaline
I snorted & dropped & smoked
Cannabis clouds floated through the Albuquerque Civic Center
A surreal hypnotic ambience as red men
Filled pipes with yellow speckled gray peyote
I puffed with them as they turned into coyotes & prairie dogs
The Fudge hit the fan like a derailed roller coaster
The bass player sawed & rammed his guitar through his amp
Making people's electrified hair stand on end
The drummer hacked away with his battle axe
At fiery dragons & demonized apparitions
It got funeral pin drop quiet
A blonde lion pranced on stage & screamed
Like ten million rats & cats on fire
Followed by a gypsy with a violin bow & a double neck guitar
A bevy of beautiful naked women danced in
Then a throbbing pulsating zeppelin hovered above
Raining down rose petals & marijuana buds
The circus became a dervish blur of flying fish & seahorses
I awoke alone & naked in a crater of an extinct volcano
Watching the stars above the Sangre de Cristos
I contemplated next weekend
Hendrix & Iron Butterfly were scheduled.

Eric Silvera

Festival

Enormous, inflatable eyeball
Shuffled slowly over our heads
Landing on the crowds' clammy palms.
Pushed up again
It drifted the horizon between
Henry Hudson's Spitting Devil and the Navajo-skinned sky.
Lady Liberty's back turned from the crowd,
Us,
No fire in her sepulcher,
As if to say
This is what you've done with everything I've given you?
Content to view the skyline,
Disenchanted by a muddy, drunk mess behind her.
A mother who brags her son attended Yale,
But bristles he's an artist instead of lawyer.

The joint really hit me.
Karen O. shifted into a black widow on stage.
I smoked with a friend of a friend
A black dude
Can't remember his name.
"WAS IT THE CURE? SHELL SHOCK!"
Music snatched my body
Saw my thighs and knees bounce –
Jerky, angular
JANGULAR.
Looking over to my drug friend
His neck rolled soulfully from side to side –
Fluid, Rhythmic
StevieWonderEsque.
As we moved together
Jagged and melodic
Our hands brushed against each other twice.
Was he trying to seduce me?
Brushed again.

It wasn't the time to be another man's fever dream.
I slushed away into a maze of Port-O-Potties
And got lost for minutes.

Escaping the smell
I found two friends
And skipped to them giggling
With hugs and forehead kisses.
They said, "You must be high."
Recent thundershowers left them shivering damp t-shirts

We began the journey to Q-Tip's stage.
Trekking through mendacious mud
We struggled to pull out feet.
It was the coagulated blood of wounded soldiers
On the field of Gettysburg and we couldn't differentiate
Between screams of the dead or cheers from fans.
I longed for days of turkey-wrapped chicken
In Central Park and her requests to sketch.
Her sea shell hips made a hell of a stick figure.

We arrived and Q-tip danced across the stage
Shaking, sliding, wailing
A modern day James Brown
A true entertainer, a real politician
I could never be a politician
My hair is thinning too early.
We smoked another joint.

Mud, Blood, Burritos.
Jay-Z, Joints, Jangular.
S.I.Ferry, Sea Goblins, Salt Shakers.

I sprawled the Fulton Street subway floor
— torn, frayed, muddy —
34th street, nobody there.
Penn Station Blues
Bring me in.

Karen Jane Cannon

Gravity

At Glastonbury we knew
our friendship was nearly over. We pitched

old squares of canvas, hammered
each rusted peg.

All around the thumping bass
of the music stages and mopeds—

Rastafarians shouting *Hash for cash!*
expertly weighing and slicing.

Our lives would soon be different.
There was nowhere left for us

except the place where everyone became
cigarette ends glowing in the dark.

All we could smell was the warm, deep musk
of hashish, the deep yearning

for something life couldn't yet give.
Tomorrow we would pack up

our lives and say goodbye.
But tonight — we stumbled, cortisol pulsing,

over crackling campfires, past tents illuminated
like paper lanterns. We clutched

each other, trying to keep
the ground beneath our feet.

Then we sat and watched the planets.
The only thing holding us was gravity.

Smoking Babbs' Weed
~ for Ken Kesey

To cruise non-intersected
through the breath
of thought, where
each one is
set perfectly clear

by the cruise itself.
It is nirvana. It is salvation.
It is awareness,
liberation, that I've
always been,
that *I truly am.*

Exaggerating the Present

We watched the animals get high
and decided to try some of what they ate.
Some of us still take a shot at bliss on catnip.
Others add a dash of oregano to the sauce.
The outcome is never the same. Sometimes we
land too hard in an exaggerated present
or try to prolong the ritual at all costs
and poison the sweet meat of everydayness.
God, did we invent you for our consciousness
to alter in the throes of religious pursuit? We fly
right around the curve and into nirvana.
The eyes gleam and imagine. An improvised
word is spoken in honor of the opioid manner.
Oh cannabis, you work on the mind
in order to borrow our feet. We plant you all over,
our sativa from terra firma, and watch
you grow to feed the heads with the Platonic ideal
. . . from China to India to the Scythians to Greece.
And now in the suburbs of the nation's great cities
there seems to be a growing trend to self-administer
like those stoner squirrel monkeys that press
the lever faithfully to get their dose of THC.
Spiders get high and stay up all night to weave
their webs haphazardly, play jazz instead —
which is how you invoke the spider gods
or at least keep them scurrying
in the great attic overhead.
Down below where the rooms fill up with
home-grown smoke, there's no reason
to worry about where all this consciousness
might wind up. Come, relax with my two dogs
and me as we exaggerate the present.

Kerry A. Bennett

Stay Present

Reality slips
Into something softer,
Like a subtle dream,
Where my perception alters
To fit
This kinder, nonjudgmental world.

I play with thoughts,
Holding them, juggling them,
And releasing them into the void.
I become amused with the chatter in my head,
Knowing it is only ego talk
And not the essence of who I am.

My stoned eyes
Encounter fellow travelers
On a journey through life
Where it becomes easy
To forgive and forget
And simply remember to be
Present
In the timeless Now.

I appreciate my place
And gratitude flows from me
Into a space where I accept
All that is
In this moment.

Jayne Martin

The Lost Years

It has only been recently that scientists have discovered that the prefrontal cortex of the brain – that crucial area that governs impulse control and decision-making – doesn't fully develop until the age of 25.

This being the case, and considering the things my underdeveloped brain thought were great ideas prior to that age, there is no rationale to explain why I'm still alive. But for some reason, like a fish so tiny you'd be embarrassed to admit you caught it, God just kept tossing me back.

The year is 1969. I'm living with a roommate near the epicenter of the "sex, drugs and rock 'n' roll" culture that is San Francisco. The décor is early-hippie chic and friends often gather here to smoke weed and consume copious amounts of Sara Lee chocolate cake.

It's a Sunday afternoon when my roommate and I decide to drop acid, hop into my Triumph Spitfire and drive out to Half Moon Bay beach to watch the sunset. We time our ingestion of the colorful drug to assure a safe arrival at our destination before our "trip" kicks in. "Knights in White Satin" blares from the 8-track as we meld into the fiery light show until the sun's final rays disappear into the blackness of the ocean. And now it's dark. Damn, it's dark. Something we had not planned on in our eagerness to stuff our cerebrum with hallucinogenics and embark on this little adventure. Or the fact that the car is now axel-deep in sand.

Around this same time, just to the east in the college town of Berkeley, many of our peers are engaged in Vietnam War protests, and images of violent clashes with police bleed nightly out of our television and into our highly-susceptible young minds. And so imagine our first thoughts when suddenly, out of the darkness, appears a group of loud, raucous youths who begin rocking my car.

As stoned as they are, they still have more working brain cells than we do and, after a quick assessment of our predicament, they are just lifting the car out of the sand. We gift them with the rest of our weed, exchange peace signs, and they disappear back to wherever they came from leaving us, once again, alone.

Neither of us is functional enough to drive. I can steer, sort of, and work the clutch. I cannot coordinate that with the gear shift. My roommate can operate the gear shift, but only when I yell, "Now!" and my timing lacks, shall we say, a certain consistency. Adding to the merriment of the evening is the fact that we have no idea which way is home, but not to worry. My still-adolescent prefrontal cortex has a plan: There are other cars on the road whose drivers all seem to know where they are going. Surely, if we just follow one of them we'll end up… someplace.

The tiny car lurches onto the highway and keeps right on lurching accompanied by intermitted shouts of "Now!" *grind,* "Now!" *grind.* We aren't exactly keeping up with the flow of traffic, so each car we start to follow almost immediately disappears and we have to choose another.

Decades later, my old roommate and I reconnect and recall the events of that night. To this day, neither of us has any memory of how we made it home. We only know that we woke up in our apartment the next day, both of us marveling at our good fortune to still be alive – and speculate that we probably lit up a joint to celebrate.

Jane James

I Did Not Inhale

Cannabis can be smoked or eaten,
the policeman told the meeting of older people,
and has a quite distinctive smell, he said,
so we can tell if someone has been using it.

With a certainly-not-suspicious look
and too-bright smile fixed on my lips
I pulled a corner of my scarf, took
a tiny, surreptitious
sniff.

Jim Fulcomer

Mary, Mary, Not Contrary

Mary, Mary, not contrary, watches her garden grow.
In little plots she raises pot. It's legal now, you know.

She hoped she'd score some prime supply, which might dispel her pain,
or just relax her frazzled nerves, she hastened to explain.

With Gro-lights, care and water and lenience of law,
our Mary had an Agribiz and got a monthly draw.

Her product was in great demand; 'twas high in THC.
The lettuce from her weed-supply increased substantially.

A full organic grower now, she wants to make it plain,
whatever you may call it, it still is Mary Jane.

The Farmer of Leeds 2.0

There was a young farmer of Leeds,
Who swallowed six packets of seeds.
    It soon came to pass
    He was covered with grass,
And he couldn't sit down for the weeds.

It was after a trip to Guiana,
He started to sprout marijuana,
    Now the farmer gets high
    Just by shaving his thigh,
And spends all of his time in Nirvana.

So Poor

> *Dad's comment after seeing...*

Four farm hands share
their hand-rolled
back behind the barn,
smells like rabbit tobacco

Peter D. Goodwin

The Wrong Indians

She had a look that pulled me towards her, the way
she held her body, her black flared dress, high
heeled boots, how she tossed her shiny black hair,
her eyes dark, shaded green, with dramatic long lashes.
Her smile was warm, open and inviting.
I was pulled into her orbit, I was enveloped
within her cone of confusing aromas
her penetrating perfume, sweet tropics, fermenting
berries, fading flowers, along with her own seductive
body scent, which would have been demonically erotic, but
for an unwelcome stale bitter smell of rancid tobacco.

My desire to kiss her dampened. That smoke created
a barrier that poisoned the air, my mood, my desire—
smoke coated not just her lungs, but her whole being
creating an invisible but impenetrable barrier
barring the life of the senses—her breadth, her skin, her hair coated,
a cancerous cataract distorting and smothering erotic possibilities.

A Pity.
Her skin was invitingly soft, I could bury my face
in her thick satiny hair, her shiny red lips inviting mine.
I thought—if only the first contact of our white ancestors
had not been with the Indians that were of the tobacco growing tribes
if only they had first met those who grew and smoked marijuana
how much sweeter she would smell, how much more
delicious she would taste, how much happier she would be
as we smoked and floated together
creating our own irresistible world, unworried
about stale smells, coughing, being busted, or about death,
just enjoying the moment, all our senses on fire, our blood
pulsating, our bodies levitating in ecstasy.

Instead my nose twitched
my throat coughed
I moved away
full of regret.

William Doreski

Cadence of the Latest Century

So I'm in the post office chatting
with the chief of police about
his model railroad featured
in *Model Railroader* magazine
and I open without thinking

the package you sent from Boston
and there's this ounce of mary jane
which I don't smoke but you sent
as a joke. Luckily the chief
had his mind on another track:

a rusty, weedy siding modeled
cleverly and photographed close-up
with a weathered New Haven boxcar
spotted by a steam locomotive
with convincing digital sound.

His beeper beeped and he dashed away
to a drug bust in the assisted
living complex where rich folks retire.
You almost retired me to prison.
Here in this greasy little town

the reek of illicit drug use
sours the cloudy light of autumn.
Politicians have to go naked
to prove their public innocence,
and realtors duck into taverns

to play the piano and sing
the rock and roll of their childhood.
We all wear the same gauzy web

and stick to it and struggle
with the same feverish cries.

The chief of police understands
he could arrest the whole village
without touching the source of crime,
the throbbing organ underground.
Tomorrow in church I'll drop

your baggie of marijuana
into the silver collection plate.
Nestled among tens and twenties
it will surprise no one, not even
the tough young woman presiding

at the altar. Like you she exudes
a faint yellow flame: hot enough
to warn of the depths, cool enough
to leave our tattoos unedited
but varnished with indelible sweat.

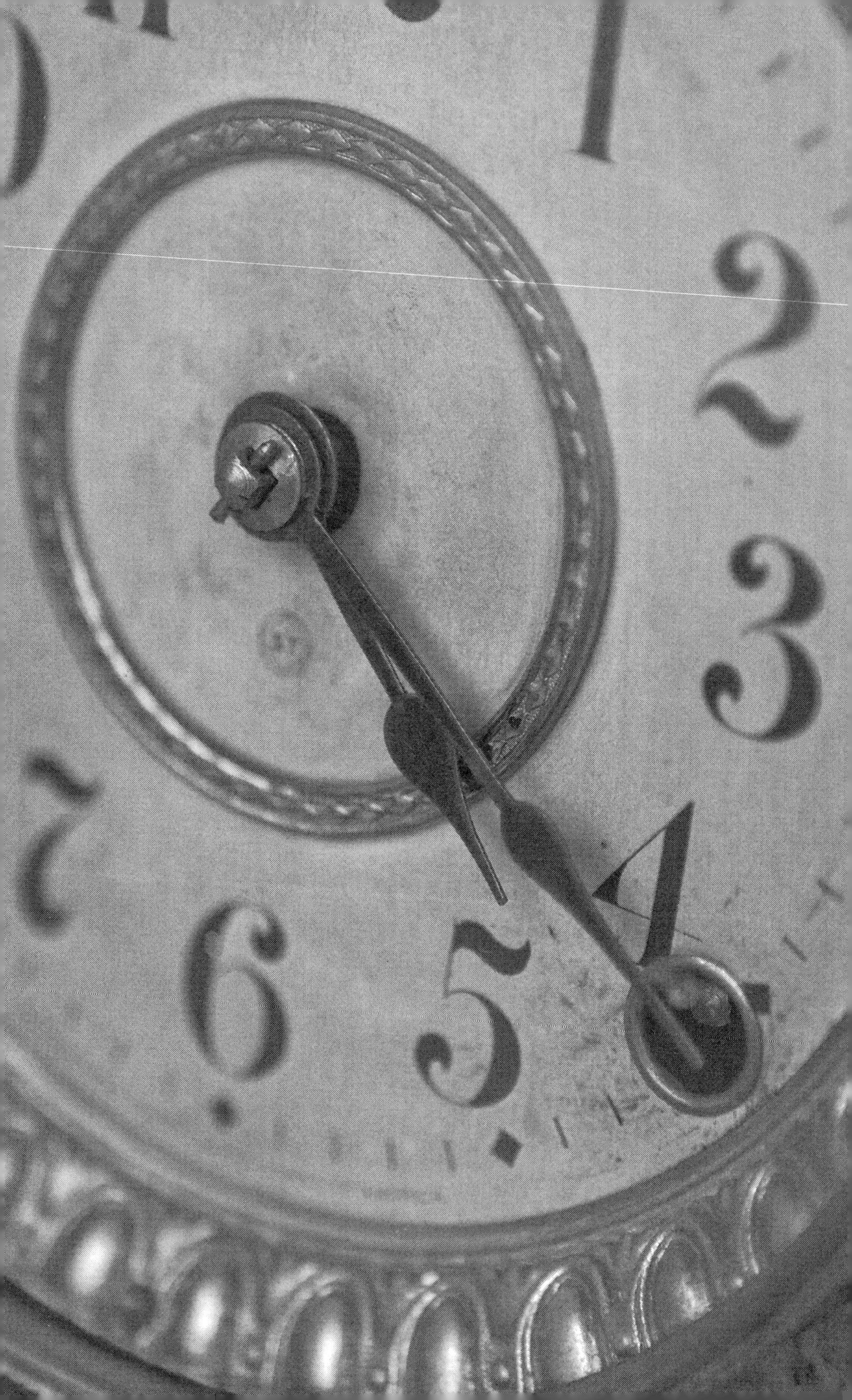

It's ... um ... 4:20

In abandoned auditorium,
a randomized consortium,
protested moratorium,
'gainst storefronts selling weed.

as majority had formed,
the um—forum, for the more of 'em,
contesting buds & bored-i-um,
lent "more blunt" telling creed ...

a dozen pot emporiums,
was edict of that quor-i-um,
their best—but I think more of 'em,
"sense" euphoria is weed

Brandyn Johnson

Oh, the Places You'll Purchase It

Etiquette

A last resort, the only one that answered so I'm here, across the street from the playground. A shared studio apartment, walls peeling, dishes shifting in the sink; his roommate shirtless, upping his online poker bet, mouth open. A quicksand recliner. *Want a cream soda?* So caught off guard by the specificity, I agree to have one. Apartment scent bullying my senses. Bacon. Incense. Sweat. Skunk. *What you want?/Eighth/He don't do eighths just grams/three grams then/alright usually people smoke with him you wanna smoke/sure I'll load a bowl/he don't do bowls just joints.* I don't like any of this. But I appreciate their help so I drive home reeking, ripped, ripped-off. Faint lingering of vanilla on my tongue.

High School

A friend of a friend of a friend got me in a room filled with cologne/B.O./skunk musk.
All boys except the one twenty-something loser that buys them booze. They act like we're competing, like I can't stop even though I've got the wavy legs. Acned hyenas cackle around me, calling one another faggots and talking about pussy.

Witnesses and Accessories

Quick and simple at a grocery store. Adjacent parking spots. Her name means "one to be wondered at." It fits. I hop into the passenger seat, money knotted in my hand. Done. Then, the soft stirring in the carseat. The pang in my gut.

Old enough to know this isn't normal. Old enough to remember a face and point it out next time they visit daddy at work. Young enough to simplify it to the *man that buys baggies of green stuff from daddy.*

Just because he doesn't care doesn't mean he should hide the fact that three generations of family are in the living room while I'm stopping by for twenty seconds. I force eye contact. I pretend I don't recognize someone who hopefully does the same.

Amateur Hour

That's it. I can throw it on the scale if you want/sure go ahead. A gram short and he doesn't know how that happens. His shaking hands make it right. They'll nickel and dime you, even with nickels and dimes.

Always

Get used to seeing guns. On the wall above the safe, on the bed, on the coffee table surrounded by shake.

Red Flag

He keeps the door to his sputtering Civic locked. With one hand he snaps the money out of mine, with the other he flings it out the window. Gone before it hit the ground, whatever was in that goddamned bag.

On Foreign Soil

American saps are the most abundant of all delicacies. They wait for the tourists — Hawaiian shirt, board shorts, taking pictures of menus, cameras like tacky medallions around their necks, muttering over and over how *authentic* everything is — to come stumbling along before the offers. *Come on, man. Good stuff. Good price.* Desperate to feel like home, I hand him a few bills. He runs away so fast it's almost funny.

If you want me to be totally honest, that happens two more times.

It's our honeymoon, after all.

Christopher Luna

Edward Albee Knew the Score

    an arousing nexus
    of sex, weed,
    and chocolate
    holds unimagined rewards
    for the brave traveler

    a far better evening for
    hardened hearts
        to be coaxed open
        the perfect moment
    to pass through the portal

        (rediscovered)

    suddenly the shrieks of children
    are indistinguishable from the birds' cry

    sorrow, laughter, and hunger
        bubble up
        to remind us
        not to die
        before we die

Jennifer Pratt-Walter

Green

It's so easy
ride that cottony dream
where magic is wearing
green and mist
that teases, heals,
makes whole
Where it spells b-l-i-s-s
written across the list
of all your sharp and broken places

Breathe that green
feel your life turn liberal
Breathe more
and your body becomes a blatant
sexual revolution

Adrian Ernesto Cepeda

Exhaling Drags

With the window cracked,
how I loved watching you inhale
like you where silently extinguishing
demons through the side of your mouth
exhaling drags with the softest thought clouds.
The way you flickered ashes, closed eyes
not even looking and never missing
always spoke to me—
like the way the cigarette would land
hanging there gently, and with every
sativa hit you silently took in
I dreamed of your hips, wanting
to float inside and letting it out
as I started rising harder
I just wanted to taste your smoky dank
tongue kiss. With every puff you silently
took in rising faster, have me thirsting dry
mouth dreaming of your lips,
wanted to float inside
jealous of the smoke that would fill your lungs;
wanting you to take me,
grip my face and exhale all the indica
clouds watching soar inside,
wishing I could be more
than the imperfect match
burning for a taste your
sticky golden trip.

Carolyn Smuts

The Pothead Lover

Impotent bastard.
You string me along,
Turn me on
With your slow hands
And smooth
Voice

But there it ends

It makes me turn to *Urban Dictionary*
Create a new word
Because
You can't
Follow through

You bong-wielding stoner,
You make me coin phrases
Like Marijuana Dick
Because you're too dulled
To fuck

Tricia Knoll

My Marriage to Merry-Jane

Overchords or underchords
of women singing to acoustic or lightweight
guitars, sway and rock-a-my-soul to comfort haze
glass pipes, licorice papers,
growlights and a stained tooth.

I plugged in lights in front of tin foil
and invoked celestial blessing beings.
I married her before gay marriage,
ballots, legality, tinctures or green crosses.
I knew brownies.

I was a spouse who loved addictions like crazy,
crazy like a dance on the Cape Cod seashore in a fish net,
when Africa slide off a map at Yale Law School,
a patient wait for starlight over Half Moon Bay.

We didn't grow apart. Or *Go different directions*
as they say. We usually went the same direction.
Once I got too crazy and all hell
broke loose. Fists flew. Concussions.
A torn ear. She knew how to make me mad.

I gave up losing my mind
bedding a budding whore
that didn't keep her promise
to be true. Severance.

After we spliff-split
she kept the ash.
I kept smoke dreams rising.

Rebecca Bilkau

Tarot Readings

The mark on the Star card is birch-bark light
though the pack is damp as autumn forests.

It's a thumb-print. Yours. Touch perfect. Whoosh.
and there you are again, you and Carmela,

blurred by separate mournings, but clear
enough to travel the ridges of grief, while rain

dog-tooths the windows, cats arch busy backs
and the child fashions tiaras from sultanas

and Plasticine, in case. You raise the card
like a shell, to hear the wet logs sizzle

in her old iron grate, the cookies steam
on her make-shift griddle, and the ploc-ploc

of the next constellation of tarots.
In the good light of now you notice the runes

on the reverse: you read them, understand
you wrote so stoned you knew the only

vital ingredient in hash cake is faith.
And you, you had your doubts; left the seeds

you posted to your own alias sealed
in the envelope franked in Irish punts;

gave up soothsaying and took up living
dangerously. Married. Still, at new moons

you sidle into the woodshed, reach, reach
into the dark, where you keep the Star,

and all the other cards, the parcel of weed
seeds and the wobbly tiara. Safe. In case.

Eileen Malone

Tea Leaf and Cannabis Reader

She greets me in her mandatory wardrobe of Goth casual black as if it were tax season and I an unexpected write-off. She sits across from me, her back to the window, looms as a dark silhouette puffing on a small ebony pipe which she passes to me.

I sniff it first to see if I want it. Yes, I do. Then I inhale the one hit she asks me to take, only the one, the prerequisite for this reading. The cannabis is rough, scratches hotly at my throat. I cough. She smiles. Pours unstrained tea into Chinese lacquer cups. Nods. I take a sip. It smells like red camellias which means like prayer-pamphlets drying after being freshly printed. Or could be messages pulled from stale fortune cookies that had pointed their corners toward me in invitation.

She asks me to say my name three times so that when I speak it, I empty like my teacup which she reaches for, claiming the leaves she studies are oolong that grow at such a high altitude Taoist monks train monkeys to pick them. I sit quietly while she studies my cup, looking into it the way a cat stares at someone or something unseen. I feel our pulses and heartbeats adjust to the steady whirring of the digital clock.

One more hit apiece, she insists. This time it is mild, easy, like her voice as she begins to speak. I want to believe her as she reverses the necessity of contradiction. Want to receive her yeasty predictions of what makes sense, makes possible seeing all the way. I want this reading to be one of never-ending examinations, not the kind buried in the language of therapy groups and twelve step programs where I was thrown a life jacket when I could already swim and anyway the water was waist high. I want to identify multiple versions of myself.

A feather-tickle of a loose cobweb prickles the back of my neck. The tea leaf reader is once again right about all that change and consolidation I accepted a life and a life ago. She addresses paths I forgot to follow that have slowly sealed. She is not wrong, no, never wrong, she explains, merely what I want to believe of what is offered.

The reading complete, she assumes the facial expression that women affect when they return to their places errorless after Communion.

The air we breath is a confession of smoke that finally realizes it came from the fire of burning buds.

Jade Ware

In the Air

Jasmin incense floating on air
We inhale and I'm almost there
Minds drifts to another place
Shotgun kiss worries erased
I hear a quintessential Marley tune
On this rainy Friday afternoon
He kissed it, Natural Mystic
Got to have kaya got to get higher
Feeling inspired light my fire, now
Spark to beautiful flame, what's my name
Rick loved Mary Jane, she adored him the same
Super star, funky guitar
He made her a full blown star
Her smoke in his eyes, they fantasize
Jah's gift to man, I'm a therapeutic fan
Legalize don't criticize, do not despise
She makes nature rise to the skies
Head in the clouds, it's where we live
Laughing out loud, puff and give
Inhale as you walk on by
Enjoy your *accidental* contact high
Eclectic scenery lush greenery
From tiny little seeds come robust weeds
Catch a fire under tropical waterfall
Slow wind, so fine, red wine, it's time
Good smoke hot romance don't choke, let's dance!

Angi Holden

Passive Smoking

Back then we shared rooms, two random students
from contrasting backgrounds, disparate experiences
thrown together by as little chance as the toss of a coin:
the quiet bookish country boy and the urban wild-child,
both keen to spread their wings, so far from family ties.
All autumn the scent of weed filled the corridors,
familiar to one, unknown to the other who, inhaling deeply,
questioned what the sweet and cloying smell might be;
who waited for his room-mate to stub out his last cigarette
and wondered why his brain flipped when he lay down to sleep.

Katy Brown

When I was your age . . .

It was the time of protests, of
far-away dominos that could fall,
gateways and choices,
love beads and tuning-in;
incense, draft cards,
and Alice B. Toklas brownies.
Freedom.

Against this background,
my life unfolded in a
decidedly eccentric,
sometimes abusive, family.

Drugs never seemed
like a good idea to me.
Mine was a clan of excesses:
too much Scotch, too many
feelings not expressed;
too many feelings expressed
at exactly the wrong time:
loss after loss drown in
the amber of a single malt.

I dreamed of escape.
But — for me, anything that promised
artificial escape was a waste of time.
Marijuana? No thank you.
It was safest for a person in
all that pandemonium
to remain alert.
Doobie? Not me.

Brad G. Garber

First and Last

Somewhere, about halfway through my college career, I teamed up with another accomplished folk singer, who had developed his own following. We became an act. I would run through a one-hour set, then he would run through a one-hour set, then we would get together for a one-hour duo act, and lay some good harmony down. By the time we were seniors in college, we had a large following and a couple of hundred people would spread out blankets on the grounds to listen to our fall and spring concerts. People would hang out and have a fun evening.

Just about this time, pot was coming into my life. I had resisted it, sort of buying into the government propaganda that one puff of the evil weed would lead one down the path to purgatory, prison time and sexual impotency. But...I had a roommate who didn't believe all of that shit. He convinced me, after an evening of too much beer, to try a toke. "Hawaiian Gold" was the name of the best weed available in Wisconsin. He scored a half ounce. This was supposed to be really good shit, man!

When my roommate offered me a hit, I was reluctant but curious. He persisted and, finally, I gave in. I had never forcibly and consciously inhaled smoke, so I was not very good at the smoking thing. I was cautious, because I did not know what might happen. Would I start seeing purple birds? Would I wake up in the morning with people laughing at my naked body? Would I die? He lit the crumpled paper with Hawaiian Gold in it and gave it to me. "Here."

I drew in some smoke and opened my lungs to the acrid stuff. Immediately, I started choking and coughing. Nothing else happened. I coughed and coughed and coughed. I waited. After about 30 minutes, I decided to go to bed. I wasn't even hungry? The whole experience had been an utter disappointment. Here, I thought I was taking a walk on the wild side, defying criminal law, becoming a desperado. Nothing. All of the build-up, followed by the nothing.

A few weeks later, when my friend offered me a replay, I was skeptical. I had an outdoor concert scheduled. It was on a lawn, next to the art building on campus, across the road from the house I rented with several other students. Right across the road! My hour set was at hand. I rose to the stage to applause. I sat on a tall chair with my trusty guitar and started singing. It was magical. The fall evening was just a little cool. The hour went by quickly and my partner took the stage.

As I stepped off stage, my roommate convinced me to walk across the street and try some more "Hawaiian Gold." I was skeptical, seeing as how nothing happened, first time around. But, he assured me that it was common to not feel much effect from the initial few hits, and that I would probably feel something if I gave it another try. So, we sat on the couch, across the street and listened to the outdoor concert through the windows. I inhaled and choked, then inhaled again and held the smoke in my lungs for as long as I could, then choked some more. I sat there, waiting, not knowing what to expect. A few minutes went by and I started feeling something weird happening. I took one more toke and started to sink into the couch. Suddenly, the room started getting smaller and time disappeared. By the time I was feeling toasted and was laughing at inane statements or ideas, it was time for me to return to the stage, across the street.

I walked across the street feeling like I was traveling through a tunnel. When I rose to the stage, to more applause, I felt that I was looking at the concert goers from inside a cave. There they were, in the soft evening light, and there I was, in the dark. I grabbed my guitar and started playing. About halfway through the first song, I started to panic, as I started stumbling around through incomprehensible chord progressions and mumbling lyrics. My stage mate and I were trying a few new songs out on the crowd and hadn't memorized all of the lyrics, yet, so we had a music stand in front of us for assistance. As I recollect, after we stumbled through the first tune (with me doing all of the stumbling), I reached out to turn a page on the music stand and tipped it over. Papers went flying across the stage and I scrambled to catch them before they flew across the venue. As I was crawling across the stage, my musical partner gazed out across the lawn and announced into the microphone, "He goes away for an hour and comes back a totally different person." A howl of laughter went up from the crowd. Apparently, it was rather obvious to most of them just what had transpired across the street.

Once I had put things in order, I settled in to play some more music. But, that proved to be a fruitless endeavor. It quickly became apparent that I could no longer remember how to play a guitar, how to sing or how to speak coherently. I had to withdraw from the stage and settle into the grass, to allow my partner to graciously finish out our joint set without the harmony parts. That was the first time I ever experienced a "high" and the very last time I smoked pot before or during a performance. Happily, my sudden idiocy was met with tacit approval by the fans. They walked up to pat me on the back or laugh with me and to share in my carnal knowledge with approving smiles and nods of the head. In my moment of utmost embarrassment, I had just earned a new badge.

Katy Brown

Crazy Enough
(a true story)

I'd been working with the group
for about a month when a new member
leaned back in her chair and observed:

You ain't never done no drugs, did ya?
Not even weed!
Why should we listen to you, then?

The opiate treatment group could be a tough crowd.
And they were right. I hadn't taken any drugs.

All I could do was tell the truth—
    A doctor doesn't have to have cancer
    to know how to treat it.
As much as I was there to learn from them,
    they were there to learn from me—
With over 30 sober years I had a few tricks to share.

And most important— folks do drugs to relax,
    get a little crazy. I'm crazy enough without drugs.

Most of them had seen me in action;
after an initial laugh, one veteran cleared his throat,
nodded sagely, and said,
She's got THAT right!

Have you?

Have you ever smoked a bowl?
Have you ever lost control?
Have you ever toked a pipe,
when the cherry was red and ripe?
Have you ever tasted herb,
and had your thoughts turn into blurbs?
Have you ever had a hit,
and said, *Man, that's good shit*?
Have you ever held a bong,
and been entranced by its song,
and mesmerized by the climbing smoke,
that you took to be your toke?
Have you ever gotten high,
and then just sat back and sigh,
and watch the time go by,
with that redness in your eye?
Have you ever been so stoned,
that you thought your head was coned,
and then laughed 'cuz it was not,
and then blamed it on the pot?
Have you ever smelled a bud
that was sticky like fresh mud
but with a smell so sweet and kind
that you couldn't wait to show your mind?
Have you ever smoked a joint
while listening to a point
that sounded so crystal clear
but somehow you didn't hear?
Have you ever been in need
of finding tasty weed
but not possessing enough cash
to acquire that happy stash?
If you have, you're not alone.

You belong in the Temple of the Stoned.
Where we worship day and night,
getting high and feeling right.
Telling stories with our friends,
the next day doing it again.
The High Priests have the kindest kind.
(the best that you can find)
It's the most serene meditation for your soul ...
Have you ever smoked a bowl?

In 1967, Mom Never Bought Paper Towels

What is that?
                        it's a toilet paper tube

What's that?
                        tin foil bowl

Pin holes
                        yeah

                        here. use your hand
                        cover it

Like this?
                        yeah. dig it

Oh fuck. My hair is burning
                        yeah wow. far out

Shit man this is groovy
I mean really fuckin' groovy

                        yeah. hey
          did you turn the engine off?

When? Wha… ? Hey. Did you see that?
Wow. Those colors

Have you ever wondered
Where all the smoke goes?

        dig this man. a beam of light will
          travel through space forever

Far out
                        yeah man. dig it

Yeah. Heavy

                                                no shit man

What's it called man?

                                                    what?

This

                                                  this what?

Your sister is really fuckin' hot

                            hey, did you turn the engine off?

The First Time

It's cool outside
but I'm breathing a sweet fire into the air
Lying on my back
I wait
never so anxious and relaxed at once
The stars are out
The moon is full
White fluffy patches pattern the sky
just floating along so calmly—
But wait
What's that I see?
An Indian chief
a leafless tree
They're all so clear quite suddenly
Not quite in awe
I understand
the mysteries of sky and land
Earth moves as one
with all the clouds
Oh god—
did I say that out loud?
I glance to left
I glance to right
How much time has passed tonight?
The others seem quite unaware
of everything that's taking place
Do they know or do they care?
And how long's this smile been on my face?

Chella Courington

Toucans & Reindeer

The day after Thanksgiving, her mother mounted the singing reindeer with flashing antlers above the toilet, and Diana filled her ears with Angel Soft. She cringed at the trappings—tinsel strand by strand on a tree turning brown, stuffed turkey again, musical chairs with cousins she saw once a year. But the holiday changed when the cousin with luscious lips like Danny Zuko handed her dried cannabis wrapped in paper. At fifteen she had no idea what lay ahead—hours waiting for vowels and consonants to catch an upward drift and tumble down before she took another drag, holding it so long she could hear toucans screech from the den below. Their big green beaks tipped in red. Her science teacher said they were tissue thin on the outside. Yet inside, honeycombs of bone. Ridges and hollows of white calcium twirling into a playground of hexagons for no one except Diana and the boy on Christmas Eve.

Tokus
(the act of passing the pipe or spliff)

Tokus is shared magic of the pipe
that plays its music in soft brown smoke,
grating the throat but calming all else;
a blanket falling on the circle of friends,
passing it widdershins and getting through days.
A magic of community, as the aches
of heartbreak or arthritis ease, borne away
on the haze of this fragrant plant we wrap
in carved pipe or fine paper.
Tokus, conjured by a bedsit wizard
whose hocus-pocus may take away sharp focus,
but replaces it with the shared comfort and warmth
of a nest, and the lullaby promise of easy sleep.

Lydia Flores

At First, It Was Just a Sleep Aid

You smell of the mistakes you haven't forgiven yourself for
Your eyes red as if the wound of insomnia has been punctured
yet you might sleep great tonight because your eyes lay low
and your blinks create a lullaby just for the dead baby
of your past that you cradle in your empty arms.
This is how numbness works, how winter frost bites
your heart and you rather not feel or feel anything
other than the weight of your living. So you inhale
until you reach your mountain peak and you're watching
your own life from the highest height in a hazy view,
your exhales are an aria singing glory to the highest
the God of your own existence.

You are floating, or laughing, or coughing
through time unaware of the war
that rages inside of your mind between
your tomorrow and your yesterday.
Everything is hilarious and you don't
even get the joke but the joke is
everything is rotting and it's not funny.
You've got the munchies you eat and eat
but the bulimics aren't laughing.

It's all a game, like twister,
 that's how it began, arrow spins
One time for tries, twice for kicks,
three times just because—
everyone else is doing it—
and continuous for habit
for excuse, for the earth
because it's all plants
and God created plants
because you need to function

because it'll ease the pain
because you just want to
until because becomes empty of reasons.
No one wins. You fall without a care and
I fall from the weight of my own limbs
trying to keep my hand on
green for you, while holding my heart up.

You buy it, you steal it, you find it
and it's okay. at least that's what they say
because there's no harm in getting high to
balance out the lows, no harm in reaching
great heights to slide back down at
rollercoaster speed with your hands up …

until you are a garden no more
you are a fence of coiled vines
and I can't see the roses in your eyes
because you are all weeds.
You call it going green.
I call it coping, you call it recreation
because life is heavy and you've got to live light
you got to get on its roller coaster ride
with the greatest drop. And you can't stop.
I can smell disaster overtaking
the perfume of your Gardenia heart
the way fog hangs in the air and you
are only wet a little bit until you come out
on the other side soaked in the things you
tried to erase. You are wilting with numbness.
I am weeping and you are day dreaming
screaming and you've turned up the heat cuz you
said you couldn't hear. giggled because when
 I said it was over between us, I sounded funny.
I can see the red sea parting in your eyes and
I prayed that love would cross it, like Moses did
staff in hand, on to the promise land—

we could've had a wedding on the sand—
but heavy they hang as the silence
between us and our memories drown
before love could make it through
because you're too high to stay awake
and so everything we are dies in your sleep.

Pattie Palmer-Baker

Dream Panther
(Marijuana Infused Reverie #2)

A panther creeps into my room
when night oozes black too thick to see through.
He slides in-between spaces of my dreams
levels his yellow gaze,
at my most hush-hush self,
pants his desire into my inner ear
and licks the whole of my inside,
grooming me for his indefinite stay.

Karla Linn Merrifield

In the Campground Alone

    A Florida moth seeks my lamplight
        flapping
    Mothra-ish against tent's nylon dome,
        tapping;
    a few feet away, a feral hog abruptly
        grunts,
    the Beast who stomps, snaps forest debris—
        cracks
    desiccated palm fronds; hoofed, tusked peril
        loiters,
    snorting until alligators, scuted, fanged,
        growl,
    hungering to mate, and I imagine *T. Rex*'s
        breath.

    The dream comes from watching *Jurassic World*
        ganga'd.
    I hear the Monsters, the Monsters
        chewing.

Casey Bush

I Smoked a Spider

It was dark I was drunk
Probably already stoned
Didn't need another hit
Like I said: Dark, Drunk, Stoned
Picked up what I thought was dried bud
But certainly it could well have been an insect
Felt the same packed into the pipe
A fly a wasp a moth a midge
In any event properly ignited
Set on fire and sucked up
Thought it was some dead leaves
A thorn a thistle an incandescent straw
Tasted like holy hemp
Could have been anything maybe even a spider
Accented by a gooey pipe residue
No use scraping the screen for a corpse
Medicinal moss fern fungus mold
Husk larvae seed pupae pulp algae
Bong fodder clogging up the old windpipe
Although upon reflection maybe it was a spider
Illuminated by flame as it danced within a blaze
Inter-digitating 8 legged arachnid-like
Bosa Nova Quick Step Samba Paso Doble
Slowly stimulated by heat
Quickly reduced to ash
Yes I may well have smoked a spider
Or some such sentient being
Animal vegetable mineral stone paper scissors
Following the long legged blond
Straight down the rabbit hole
Gobbled up by obligatory prescriptions
Unexpected tax refunds
Highways lined with salad bars

And the fumes of flesh
Casting clouds of doubt
Upon preconceived notions
About the allegedly vast differences
Between the plant and animal kingdoms
Ultimately satisfying and oh so smooth
Got high while an insect did its last heel and toe
Got me thinking maybe it's the next big buzz
As yes I guess I actually smoked a spider.

The Erratic Train

Feel the paranoid, ride the erratic train
as you sit around a black coffee table
in a duplex apartment in Saint Johns.

Pass the joint to Michael on my left,
his black fingers still stained with blood,
ancient remnants of the murders committed
for heroin and cash, 25 years inside.

He lifts the end to his lips and sucks it in,
holds his breath, for 30 seconds, exhales
the musky smoke to the jagged ceiling.
then he hands it to Norman,

who squints his black Cuban eyes, as he
inhales, I can almost see the skeletal
finger bones glisten white beneath brown skin
as his skeleton lips part, and he smiles
passes the disappearing joint back to me.
he was stabbed to death by three Mexicans
as he drunkenly lurched down Lombard.

Two middle aged men smoke grass
with a sixteen-year-old boy in St. Johns.

But right now, I don't give a fuck.
I have a home grown permagrin.

At least at first, but I'm riding
the erratic train with a convicted murderer
and a future homicide, feeling paranoid.

Every goddamn time a car rolls by outside

I look out the window, eyes peek out
between two dusty white blind flaps,
as I know the cops will come, bust me
when they see my bloodshot eyes,
smell the wasted remains of cannabis
upon my faded blue denim jacket,
listen to my emphatic denials lazily drift
from the surface of my stoned tongue.

I ride the erratic train
with a convicted murderer
and a future cold case homicide.

Trippin'

"Hey Johnny Boy! Get over here you lame-ass burnout!"

Pete Culbertson. What an *asshole*. What in the hell does *he* want?

I was just about to enter the Qwik-Mart to address a serious case of The Munchies. Fuck, was I baked. Nevertheless, I turned around and sauntered up to his late-model jet black Mustang convertible. Pretty damn cool car, actually, I gotta admit.

With the top down on this warm and sticky summer night, I could see that he had two sidekicks with him.

"Climb on board my Pony, jackoff. We need you to see something. Gonna blow your shit right away, man."

'Why me, Petey?"

"'Cuz you were Pre-Med, man. That is until you dropped out of State. And we need an expert medical opinion. Or at least as near as we can get. So come *on*. We got a trip to take, John-oh. Now get your *ass* in the car!"

Okay. First of all, I was a *Marine Biology* major. Yeah, that's pretty close to Pre-Med there, ass clown. Still, the dude had now definitely captured my interest.

"All right, Pete. I'll come with you. But I'm driving my own car. I'll follow you."

Petey boy was *really* haulin'. Easy now, Speed Racer, or you're gonna lose my lame-ass '99 Camry. Suddenly, the streaking 'stang swings a wicked hard left, and a few seconds later comes skidding to an abrupt halt. Then he and Bert and Ernie leap out of the Mustang and take off running toward a cluster of trees, motioning for me to follow. No sooner did I take a cautious step in pursuit then Pete starts making like a damn Tasmanian Devil, spinning on a dime and pointing emphatically and repeatedly to the ground near a big-ass old oak tree.

"*Look! Look at that!* Lying right *there!*" Pete urged, pointing to what appeared to be a large bump next to the tree's thick trunk.

"We were just hangin' out, chillin', drinkin' and tokin', right? And Jeremy here trips over somethin'. And it's this fuckin' dude! And he's *dead!*"

I was just about to open my mouth and utter words I'm sure were going to be most profound, then suddenly I jumped back.

"*SHIT!* The fucker just *MOVED!*"

Twisting his torso in a rocking motion back and forth, he began to rise. From the waist at first. And then to his knees. Eventually he stood, motionless, staring at us staring right back at him. Suddenly, and without warning, the vertical corpse took a slow but sure step *toward* us.

We were about to turn tail and get the hell outta Dodge when we hear this voice. "Hey! Guys! Hold on, man! I'm not dead! I'm *ALIVE* for crissakes!!"

We all four stopped dead in our tracks. So to speak.

Slowly, warily, we turned around and gazed in the direction of this creepy-ass voice.

"I have this thing where sometimes I just fall asleep. Wherever I am. With no fuckin' warning at all."

"Oh, wow." blurts out one of Pete's partners. "You mean like necrophilia and shit?"

"No, dumb ass.", I scoffed. "That's when you fornicate with dead people. He's got *narcolepsy*. Right, man?"

That's correct. I'm talking with a guy I'm still not convinced isn't dead. Once again, cut me some slack. I'm fried.

"Yeah, that's right. Have been since I was a kid."

"So what in the hell are you doin' lyin' out here under a tree?" I inquired.

"Okay. I guess I owe ya." he conceded sheepishly. "So I had this date tonight with this *really* hot snatch. We go to this nice Italian place downtown. A little pasta. A lotta wine. And she starts gettin' all friendly. 'Oh, you're so funny. I just *love* a guy with a sense of humor.' Shit like that. And I'm optimistic about where this night might ultimately end up goin' here. Finally, she's like, 'Hey. Can you take me home now?' And I'm like, 'Check please', right? So we split the restaurant and hop in my car. Which, by the way, did you guys happen to notice a dark blue Beemer in the vicinity by chance?"

"Yeah. It's parked on the shoulder of the road about a half mile that way" I responded, pointing toward the main road.

"Lazarus" started to walk away, but I shouted after him:

"Hey! So did you bang her or what?!"

"Shit, *no*, man. Turns out the chick shares a condo with her brother. An MMA fighter. And the fucker was *home*. She asked me to come in for a nightcap, but now anticipating no pay-off, I declined. It was sayonara and a dry dick for me, dudes."

"Bummer.", I replied. "But that still doesn't tell us why in the hell you were lying out here in the fuckin' forest like this?"

"Oh, you wanna talk about 'Blue Balls', man. So I pull over on my lonesome ride home, get out of the car and march out into these woods. And then, just as I was about to unbuckle and whip it out to yank away my massively pent-up frustration, here comes my ol' buddy 'Mr. Sandman'. *BAM!* And the only thing I wind up slammin' is the turf, baby. Now, aren't you glad you asked? Ha-ha-ha!"

And with that candid confession, he was gone, laughing into the night.

After bidding goodnight to Pete and his posse, I got back to my trusty 'yota and instinctively scoured the ashtray in search of a "live" roach. Releasing a huge-ass exhalation of relief, I addressed myself out loud, "One of these days we're gonna get our shit together and get off the grass, Big John." I uncovered a junior joint in my ashtray, sparked the sucker on up and raised the burning butt to my lips. As I drew in a hellacious hit, I declared with bated breath:

"However, today would definitely *not* be that fucking day."

Personal History

The reason I gave up
smoking dope
the little people,
the ones disguised as oversized
potato bugs.
They always showed up
around midnight,
scared the piss out of the dog —
me too.

David Belmont

David Lerner: One for the Holidaze

Backstory

My parents had a circle of political friends, all Jewish communist couples with children: the Lerners, the Kelmans, the Kreuters. All the families lived in Queens. We lived in Astoria, right across the river from Manhattan, while the Lerners (Flushing), Kelmans and Kreuters (Bayside) lived further out, closer to Long Island. All the families had three children with the oldest (all boys) being born within nine months of each other in 1951/52.

I am the oldest Belmont child, David was the oldest Lerner child. I looked up to him as a kind of unreachable, not totally desirable role model through the 1960s. He was big (eventually grew to about 6' 3"), lanky and brusque. He sported a biting wit and a sardonic sense of humor, both well beyond his years. He turned me on to Bob Dylan, whom we idolized.

David was a trailblazer. He was hanging out in Greenwich Village, smoking weed and popping pills, before he turned thirteen. He was listening to Miles Davis and Chet Baker while we were watching the Beatles on Ed Sullivan.

David was never a hippie. He was more of a beatnik, like a character in a Kerouac novel. He kept his hair relatively short, wrote poetry, read William Burroughs and Hubert Selby, Jr., played a soulful, simple unaccompanied blues harp on a whim.

Story

It was Thanksgiving 1967. As was the tradition at the time, the families gathered at the Lerners' house for the big meal. There were seven of us mid-teenagers at the table. After the main course, we excused ourselves and retired upstairs to David's room. The centerpiece of the room was a square white marble top table that was perpetually populated by piles of books and record albums.

We were frantically chatting away when, without warning, David cleared the table with one stroke of his right arm, sending the books and discs crashing to the floor. He pulled his carved wooden stash box from the shelf behind him and placed it on the naked tabletop. He opened the box and extracted an impressive looking block of opiated black hash, a standard silver Zippo lighter, a single-edge razor blade and a safety pin. With the help of the razor blade, he broke off a large chunk of hash from the block. He then massaged the chunk into a ball, straightened the safety pin, and attached the ball to the point of the pin. While holding the hub of the pin, he lit the ball on fire with the Zippo. Once he got it going, he extinguished the lighter and let it flame on its own for about fifteen seconds. He then blew out the flame, inhaled a large drag and passed the smoking ball of hash to me. I took a toke and passed it to the guy next to me.

Our once furious conversation was now reduced to loud inhales, slurps to keep the smoke in, and some coughing, while the hashish made its way around our circle several times. It stayed smoking on its own, never requiring a re-light. After many minutes of this, we were spent and silent…and really high. David spoke up: "That was some *serious* hash smoking!" We all laughed hysterically.

Postscript

I continue to enjoy the pleasures of cannabis, to no deleterious effect (as far as I can tell), with a preference for sativas and sativa-dominant hybrids.

David moved to California in the early 70s. I visited him a couple of times during the decade, but lost touch with him after that. In 1998, I asked a private investigator friend to do a database search for him (this was before civilians could do such things by themselves on the internet). She found a recent address that turned out to be a drug rehab center in San Francisco. I called and asked for David. The guy who answered the phone said that David was no longer there, that they didn't give out any info on people, but that I could write a letter and they would forward it, if they had an address for him. I sent the letter, not expecting a reply. The following year, we did another search and learned that David had died in July 1997.

I've periodically tried to find him on the internet over the years, to no avail. While doing research for a novel earlier this year (2015), I googled "David Lerner poet" and found some relevant hits, including a Wikipedia page. The photo sent chills down my spine and prompted tears. Turns out he was almost famous. He was a leading light of the Café Babar poetry scene in San Francisco in the 80s. The Babarians, or the "new beats" as they were dubbed in the local media, were a folk art kind of expression, featuring street poets who lived on the margins. David co-founded Zietgeist Press, which still publishes the work of the Babar poets, some of it recent.

D. Russel Micnhimer

In Reference to Shakespeare's Sonnet 76** and Recent News*

Dear Bill, sir, we know now you did not eat pills
But preferred sweet smoke of burning weeds
To provoke new lines and ward off still quills
For in your pipes we found residue of seeds.
Of course t'was but mere exotic habit in your time
No one in authority came 'round to bust down doors
Laws had not been invented yet to make it a crime
Preferences were not societal matters, only yours.
Knowing minds suspected that is what you meant
Because of your many sly twists of casual words
Peregrinations to make better fit when they were bent
Evoke duplicitous meanings when they were heard.
Again in this enlightened state we the right have won
So dear Avon Bard please join us for a toke in Oregon!

*Scientists have discovered that 400-year-old tobacco pipes
excavated from the garden of William Shakespeare contained cannabis,
suggesting the playwright might have written some of his famous works while high.

**
SONNET 76
    Why is my verse so barren of new pride?
    So far from variation or quick change?
    Why with the time do I not glance aside
    To new-found methods and to compounds strange?
    Why write I still all one, ever the same,
    And keep invention in a noted weed,
    That every word doth almost tell my name,
    Showing their birth and where they did proceed?
    O, know, sweet love, I always write of you,
    And you and love are still my argument;
    So all my best is dressing old words new,
    Spending again what is already spent:
        For as the sun is daily new and old,
        So is my love still telling what is told.

Adrian Ernesto Cepeda

Reaching Back with Each Drag

Although ashes remain
sometimes
you've got to relight the end
to actually burn forward—
inhale her closer
when grasping the flame
by exhaling smoke
these clouds that transcend
floating to hide
will no longer refrain.

Alec Solomita

I've Walked Down

I've walked down this uneven brick sidewalk
in bright December, in springtime splendor,
in evening dress, unshaven, unshorn, balding
and drunk, slick and slim, smooth and sober,
in t-shirts and cargo shorts on closing summer nights.

I walked up a similar sidewalk, buckling,
reddish brick, the heart of old
Boston, where I first smoked grass forty-eight
years ago in a tiny apartment with a skinny
blonde who assured me that one of these times
I would feel it. And she was right. I feel it now
as an old man, high as a kite (the bird, not the toy)
looking down on my own life, my only prey.

Devin Taylor

Temporal Pastoral

Garage sale season's here again. Spring cleaning, soul
searching. Brought every closeted speck of substance—
found cliché memories, fond memories of
clichés—pawned them at the corner
store. My sentimental Tupperware, while limited edition crystal
clear, aint worth shit. "Fool's gold," the shopkeeper called it.
Suspected as much. But he gave me a participant ribbon
and couple of consolation dollars,

so I bought some silence and a dime bag, and
went outside to air fresh grievances, smoke
a joint, hangout the remnants of my past
epiphanies to dry. Reflection is refraction. Thoughts
change direction, The corner store's sign said "We Buy,
Sell, Trade the Used." Forecast claims tomorrow's a nice day.
I think I'll ride my bi—
Cycle.

Fractured

Astonishment visceral fractured
my ego as well as
>	my ankle
seeing my foot
>	flap
caught me on the hop
if not my body – then who?
On my back
>	in lethal grass (wet)
something cracked me deep
people whispered into mobiles
covered me with blankets
>	while I numb
someone screamed *'Fuuuuck!'*
>	me I think.
After the repairs, the pain;
neighbours shopped, friends
fetched me back to bipedal health
but something
>	cracked me.
Don't know what it means.
>	*'It's aging'*, I said
>	*'It's having a body'*, said Geoff
quaking us into that crazy Zen laugh
we used to do in the 70s when
>	not knowing was a gas
when perception uncaged
realities like fractals
before our,
>	yes sometimes stoned
sometimes enlightened
>	eyes.

We hung out
        in that wide blue
edgy   space
cackled like loons
at the absurdity
        and brilliance
of being a Rachael or
doing a Geoffrey
before the safety bars sprang
        up like wheat.

Burky Achilles

Saturday Night, Upcountry Maui

We wind up at the slaughterhouse
because it is 9:30 at night
in a one-lane cow-town where Komoda's
closes at six, locking
their Cokes behind bars.

We are in laugh
with our girlish selves singing
Superstition in the Land Cruiser,
radio up, windows down,
tires humming.

You had the golden
ticket—Kona Gold *is* a winner—
we partook while winding
Upper Kula Highway, believing
in things we don't understand.

We suffer—you lust
for that son of a cowboy
and I long to follow the thicket
of your braid past the lip
of your hip-hugging bell-bottoms.

We are sixteen and parched,
but the slaughterhouse Coke machine
swallows my last quarter,
fingered from the pocket
of my pin-whale cords.

Under new moon, we
are so lit. Laughter rolls
as we finger each other's

thoughts, no ambient light
to smudge our inky logic.

My thighs, no eyes, unbraid
you, plait by raucous plait, until
only buttons fill the holes between us.

Halee Kirkwood

Lovesong

When my mouth sparks like the end of a spliff
on a Saturday night, my belly will be bright
with a half dozen doughnuts glazed like the moon
glows. This is how I beg to remember, I spin
my brain together like a Saturday night.
I pinwheel out of myself, out of the things I hate.
This is how I stretch myself pretty
in a carnival mirror. This is how
I don't have to remember:
boarding the bad on a neon-toothed scrambler
so the things I hate (the me I hate) smash out of themselves
and amalgamate. I give myself a sticky-fingered childhood
when I'm glazed, luminous, neon-toothed,
re-mixed and scrambling my mouth, my heart,
my spliff on a Saturday night.

Marj Hahne

Ne – Neon 10

One time when my old friend Kerrie got high, she and her pals drove aimless miles through rural Tennessee, the way high school kids with nothing better to do might do. They got lost, so Kerrie called her older sister, Linda, on a gas-station payphone for directions back home. When Linda asked her dazed-out sister where they were, Kerrie looked skyward at the giant neon Shell sign, its "S" shorted out. I don't know how long it took her to get reoriented, but that was the last time Kerrie smoked dope.

I'm one of the rare post-'60s coming-of-agers to never have toked up. I blame Clista Harvey. She came to school every morning with pot breath, and when she spoke to me, I contracted my nostrils and throat from the inside, because turning my head would've been rude. I imply that the *odeur* forever nauseates me, but the truth is, I was an obedient and ambitious child: marijuana was illegal, and I didn't want to break the law. I wanted to go to college. A good one. I wanted, forever, to get the hell out of that town.

Free 99

    strawberry swishers
        white owls
    black & mild's
        five finger discount
    count the number of
    blunts back to your
    innocence & count the
    number of transactions
    chopped into lines
    with your credit card
    back to when your
    wallet didn't smell
    pharmaceutical &
    realize that maybe
    you actually aren't
    that bad at math &
    maybe your soccer
    coach calling you emo
    was a compliment
        Rust-Oleum
    Krylon
        Kilz
    all that can fit in your
    led zepplin world tour
    hoody in some middle
    of Ohio Walmart count
    the cost of the potential
    misdemeanor count the
    minutes it takes for the cops
    to turn the corner count the

number of hours before
the sun will rise count
the wishes for it not to
count the miles between
Cincinnati & Denver

Teresa Zemaitis

Smoke Screens

Megan wakes slowly every day. She has to.

Sometimes it's instant. The pain that twists her stomach and starts the violent retching that can last for hours, days even. Sometimes it's lazy, a weakness that builds to the nausea. Some days she gets lucky and does not have to run to the bathroom to grab her Zofran. Those days give her a little time. Time to take the anti-nausea medication before it starts. Time to take the hydrocodone elixir before the pain begins while she can still keep it down.

Diagnosed three years ago, at 21 years of age, with gastroparesis, Megan suffered attacks for years. Attacks that would land her in the hospital for a couple of days, once for two weeks.

"That time was really bad," said Megan. "They were going to put in a feeding tube and a PICC line [a permanent IV] so I could take all my meds intravenously because I couldn't keep anything down—not even water. I was so dehydrated.

"A nurse came to check on me in the middle of the night. My girlfriend, Ashlee, was holding my hair back while I threw up in the barf bag. The nurse said 'Do you smoke?' with a funny expression on her face. I knew she meant pot. I said yes. She asked me if I had any and I was like 'Well, not on me right now.' She laughed and then whispered, 'If you get some, I'll prop open the side door for you. But if you get caught you're on your own.'"

Ashlee went to retrieve a blunt from her car. They went to the designated smoking area, deserted because it was 2:00 am, smoked, and returned to the room unnoticed. Megan was served a liquid breakfast later that morning, kept it down, and, after two weeks in the hospital, was discharged that afternoon.

* * *

On November 4th, 2014 voters in Megan's home state of Florida had a chance to make medical marijuana legal. Amendment 2 needed a 60% majority to pass. Megan was hoping to get a card.

She voted in the afternoon after smoking a blunt. "It's become a tradition," Megan laughed after admitting that she has used marijuana recreationally since high school. She texted all her friends that day to remind them to "vote for pot."

Halloween leftovers in hand, Megan plops down on the couch and turns on BayNews9 to watch for the results a bit before 8 pm. She wears a combination of leather and rubber bracelets that almost cover the tree of life tattoo on the inside of her right wrist, one of seven tattoos on her body.

The ticker rolls across the bottom of the screen. With only 3% of precincts reporting Amendment 2 was 58% in favor. "Ooh—it's almost 60%!"

At 8:00, with 44% of precincts reporting, the vote was down to 56% in favor. "I'll keep smoking anyway, but it would be nice to not have to worry about it."

* * *

Gastroparesis is a condition that causes your stomach to function improperly. Normally, the muscles in your stomach contract, pushing food through your digestive system. With gastroparesis, the muscles are weak or don't work at all causing your stomach to hold food longer than it's supposed to which causes nausea and, ultimately, vomiting. Lingering food can ferment and allow harmful microorganisms to grow. There is no cure for gastroparesis and many of medications used to treat the condition can cause serious side effects.

It took almost three years to diagnose Megan. She has undergone MRIs, CAT scans, a HIDA scan to test her gall bladder, a gastric emptying test, colonoscopies, EEGs, a laparoscopy, numerous endoscopes, and pints, if not gallons, of blood work. She wonders what all this is doing to her. "I've had so many x-rays, so much radiation, and that stuff they inject for contrast, the things I've had to drink to follow my digestive tract—that stuff can't be good for you. Not so many times. My medical file was 542 pages a year ago. I'm sure it's over 600 by now."

Megan has been prescribed Reglan (which caused twitching), Promethazine, Dicyclomine, Bentyl, Zofran, hydrocodone elixir, Xanax, Omeprazole, Protonix, Keppra, and domperidon (not available in the U.S.). Every trip to the emergency room means more rounds of morphine or dilaudid.

"It's so much easier to just smoke. It has to be better for me than all these other meds," said Megan. "Smoking gets rid of all the pain and nausea. If I'm only a little nauseous, the Zofran will help, but it doesn't make me hungry. At least when I smoke, I actually eat."

* * *

The election results kept rolling across the bottom of the screen. At 8:34, with 59% of precincts reporting, it was still holding at 57% in favor. It remained 57% in favor at 9:12.

Megan stepped away and returned with a package of 4 Kings Watermelon Cigars, a plastic bag containing weed, a purple pot grinder, and a Zen blunt roller.

She removed a cigar from the package, unpeeled it like a pro, dumped out the tobacco, and wet the edge of the blunt wrap, her upper lip gently dabbing the top while her tongue licked the bottom. She inserted the wrap into the green vinyl of the roller. She pulled some weed from the baggie, placed it in the grinder, twisted the cap two times, and tapped the ground herb between the rollers, gently using her fingertips to get all the "shake."

As the precincts reporting increased, Megan's chatter lessened. At 9:32 a Breaking News Alert flashed on the screen. With 82% of the precincts reporting, they declared Amendment 2 defeated. It remained at 57%, just shy of the 60% needed to pass. Megan sighed and stood up. "Guess I'll have to stay a criminal and keep leaving these on my night stand so I'm ready for the mornings."

Sarah White

The Pipe, the Plants, and the Misdemeanor
A Pantoum of '72

Little pipe in the pocket of his corduroy trousers!
He's 11. We live in Ann Arbor.
Wishing I were a wiser mother,
I ask him to explain what I found in the hamper.

He's 11, and the town of Ann Arbor
throbs with marches and teach-ins. I'm writing a thesis on King Arthur.
When I ask him to explain what I found in the hamper,
"Don't worry Ma," he says, "I've been trying to cut down."

I march and I teach-in. I write pages on King Arthur.
I let the kid keep his plants on the windowsill.
"Don't worry Ma. I've been trying to cut down."
Possession here is subject to a five-dollar fine.

He keeps his spindly plants on the windowsill.
At times, he lights a leaf in the pipe in the park.
Possession here is subject to a five-dollar fine.
One evening, as I write the dissertation,

a leaf is aglow in the pipe in the park,
and a couple of cops pick him up, bring him home.
They find, not a woman working on her dissertation,
but a mother and a boy they will charge with possession.

A couple of cops pick him up, bring him home
with a pipe in the pocket of his corduroy trousers
and his educated mother in flagrant possession.
He's a minor. She is old enough to be a wiser mother.

She owes five dollars to the Town of Ann Arbor.

Jill Hawkins

Stolen Dances

driving to my hometown
I can't help but pause and shake my head
at the places the Baptist have
burned down

no more dancing feet and swaying hips
bottles clanking and raveled cut offs
love affairs and wasted pay
checks, darkened to silence

now where will girls meet G.I.s
learn to drink for free
find mastery long before menopause
leaning back on sinks to zip up
tight fitting jeans and puff, puff, passing
the band's bongo weed

never knowing
that flirt of disaster
the two steps that led me out
the altar call of a waltz

Helen Sparrow

Smoked Out

It was a blind date at my best friend Eileen's. Her boyfriend Will brought a guy for me. I didn't catch his name, and as we ate the rice and enchiladas Eileen had made, the two of us didn't exchange a word.

While Eileen was in the kitchen getting dessert, Will dug out a box of cigarettes and looked at me.

"You smoke?"

"Oh, no, she doesn't." Eileen smiled apologetically at him as she slammed a tray of flan on the table.

He looked from me to his friend and back again.

"You two ought to get along fine."

Then he took two cigarettes out of his box and handed one to Eileen. She sniffed it and got a goofy smile on her face.

They lit up, and before too long the room was filled with a sick-sweet scent and maniacal laughter that a smoker's daughter knew you just didn't get from regular cigarettes.

Will's friend went bug-eyed. He stayed that way for a full thirty seconds before leaning into my ear and whispering, "Would you like to, um, get out of here?"

We didn't bother with the elevator—we charged down six flights of stairs, passing or colliding with more than a few puzzled people going the other way. When we stopped to catch our breath in the lobby, we saw rain coming off the eaves in great torrents, and I realized that in my hurry to vacate Eileen's apartment, I'd forgotten my coat. Without saying a word, Will's friend swept his off and wrapped me in it. He put an arm around my shoulders, and we stepped out into the downpour together. Two blocks later we bought crêpes from a particularly perseverant street vendor and took them under the striped awning of a sandwich shop to eat.

His name was David, he told me. He taught high school history, loved Cherry Coke, and couldn't play tennis to save his life.

We laughed the night away, crêpe coating running down our sleeves and cleaving to the corners of our mouths. It was one o'clock by the time he asked me where my apartment building was, and quarter to two when I finally dredged my key out of a skirt pocket.

After I went in, he stayed on the threshold, foot serving as a doorstop. Just as I was about to shrug out of the garment he had been so kind as to loan me all evening, he said, "I'll be by for my coat tomorrow. And don't you dare wash it."

Then he smiled at me and went to gallantly brave the rain in his sweater.

* * *

Sometime later, we learned that while we were sleeping off that first night of crêpes, Eileen and Will had gone out and tied the knot. And so, in due time, we gave them the best wedding gift we could think of.

We both voted to legalize pot in the next election.

Marilyn Stablein

After the Law Changed

You mean I don't have to sneak a toke
on the deck or in the garage or alley
during lunch break, horde peppermint
breath mints, scented air freshners,
    and incense sticks?

You mean I don't have to cower
next to the open bathroom window
of a three story walk up
with the exhaust fan on high
    any more?

You mean I don't have to hide
the papers, pipe, roach clips
and stash in a red Chinese Lichee
tea tin in a high cupboard, freezer
    bag or leather pouch?

You mean I don't have to pick twigs
out of a matchbox full, sprout seeds
in a cardboard egg carton, transplant
seedlings between corn stalks or under
    a grow light and wait for months?

No more "Drop it!" or "Freeze!"
No frisking, strip search, bust or jail time?
There are menus? High grade strains?
Fixed prices? Free samples? Tinctures?
    Candy? Pot brownies to go?

Leah Mueller

Northwest Soma

Medical cannabis storefronts
dot Sixth Avenue
like illuminated ships.
The sturdy doors are
embellished with
crudely painted green crosses
which offer relief
from chronic pain,
and neon signs flash
tantalizing messages, like
"six dollar grams"
and "purple kush special."

Some of the blocks
have turf wars
between medical
and recreational marijuana,
and the two storefronts
sit beside each other
like opposing sports teams
waiting to compete
on the field of capitalism.

The state vows to shut down
the medical cannabis outlets
because they don't pay taxes,
but the owners are shrewd
and get legal injunctions
so they can stay open
for a few more months.

On the corner of
Sixth and Proctor
one of the medical
cannabis employees
smirks and says to me
repeatedly, "Stay medicated!"
then gives me a free half-gram
to help with the process.

Meanwhile, in Texas,
people can still get life in prison
for marijuana brownies.
Guess I won't be moving there
any time soon.
It's worth putting up
with the rain.

Shawn Aveningo

Ivy and Weed

Annie grew up back east,
in one of those hundred-year-old
ivy-embossed stone houses
that make the perfect backdrop
for Christmas card photos
at the season's first snow.

Did she know?
Did anyone know
the Bostonian tendrils—snaking their way up
the north façade of her childhood home—
harbor a secret,
the most dreaded parasite of our time?

Under this leafy green cloak of charm,
Hedera Helix serves as basic training
for a malignant neoplasm invasion—
Cancer.

I imagine miniscule scarab carcinoma
marching up & down, back & forth,
under camouflage foliage,
lacing up teeny black boots, loading
tiny ray guns to combat radiation blasts,
and learning to build dams
to block the intravenous deluge
of human designer chemicals.

After nine weeks of training,
each Cancer is assigned a duty station.
One soldier goes AWOL,
hitches a ride in Annie's luggage
on her way to her new life in Cali,

where she plants *English Ivy*
—clippings she brought from home—
alongside a row of *Purple Hindu Kush*
beneath her kitchen window, so
she can bake 'special' brownies
for her father.

His lack of appetite makes it difficult
to stomach his constant side effects,
as the cancer now feasts upon his bones.
And stockholders of a pharmaceutical empire
refuse to invest in 'progressive' research,

while both the disease
and a remedy
continue to grow,
right under their noses.

John Lambremont, Sr.

Lefty

Only one white mouse
in the great lab cage
quit the nicotine spigot,
sniffed but once at the cocanoid,
hated the taste of alcohol,
and avoided like plague the opioid,
instead preferring the cannabinoid
and the mellow glow he so enjoyed.

They all called him Lefty,
for the cannabis spigot
was the one to the far left,
also in joking reference to
the left-handed cigarettes
that humans like to roll
and smoke.

All of the cool mice
hung around sipping nicotine,
and more than occasionally cocaine,
but these made Lefty feel jumpy;
and on his one try of coke
he thought he'd had a heart attack.
The sad mice drank ever-clear
or dabbled in smack,
but booze led to hangovers,
and H left Lefty's bones wracked;

so he sucked on the pot spigot
alone, without company,
and while sometimes it seemed
he was perpetually hungry,

his food pellets always
were taken as tasty;

and on the off days,
when the spigots were closed,
he would watch the other mice
run nervous in nicotine fits,
shiver with quivers and shakes,
undergo horrible withdrawals,
or suffer the *delirium tremens*,
but Lefty would stay
as calm as he pleased,
knowing that in another day
he would savor more extract
of his beloved sweet leaf.

Karen Robiscoe

Barack O's Toback'O

Bush hated Broccoli
and cursed the florets—
—on nationwide news
as bad as it gets …
but Barack
favors flowers
from Bushes in Colly!
Barack-Colly's
flower
—is better, by golly!

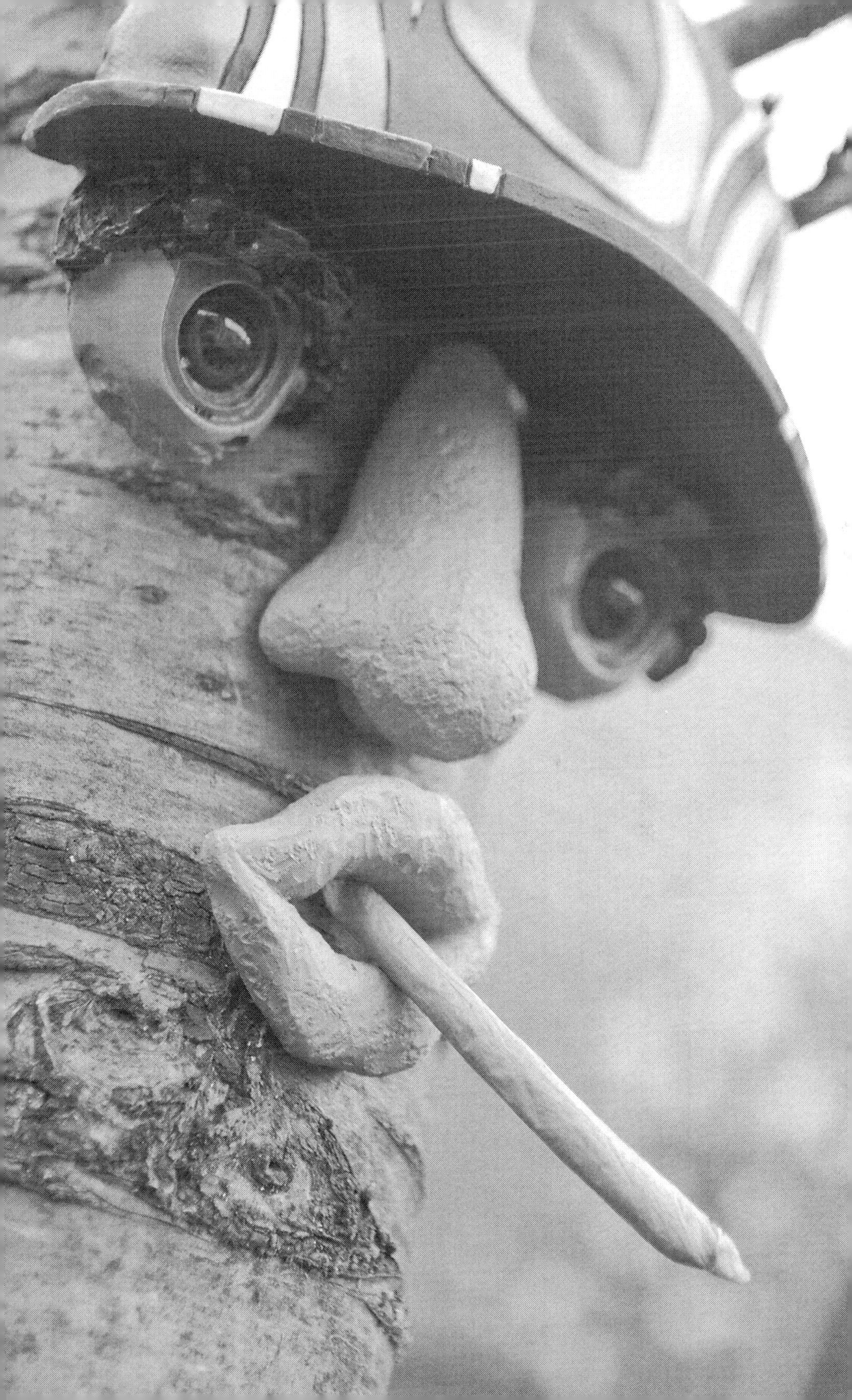

Art Goodtimes

CannaBaloney

"Don't do Pot. Your brain will rot."
~ anti-drug slogan

You hamburgers!
McRedeye sez
just like my three-pack-a-day Dad did

The Bay Area gardener
who ranted how pot
was the gateway to heroin

But ended up growing primo bud
for his next door neighbors
A lesbian couple

who had him over for dinner
Invited him out on dates
especially for sushi

It didn't make them sick
It made them
friends

Judith Skillman

Lost to Regulation

I recall the young dark-haired woman behind glass as at a teller's window,
asking for my ID and the paper that would let me pass
through the door to where, hanging from the walls, in bouquets in jars
on countertops, and beneath, crowded into shelves, the cannabis
in all its myriad forms—ointment, cream, patch, joint, tincture—
was for sale to me and me alone, as I, the only one at this moment
in the medical marijuana store, its frosted windows haloed
from the outside as if it were a Christmas shop in old London,
or a whorehouse from the old West, sat on a street in Renton
labelled with its green cross. That cross hardly stood out between
the barber and the vet. Behind the parking lot a row of mobile homes,
where people lived in the kind of poverty unimaginable to those
who have enough. Strangely, the potions never worked as much
magic as the young woman, who always said "Hi Judith,,
how are you today"? And who smiled as if she were high—
but not on Mary Jane, rather on this little job she'd snagged, coveted
no doubt by others who longed to be in proximity to the forbidden
substance I and a few others, by virtue of our pain, had gained
temporary license to enjoy. And when I left for the last time,
I told her: "I will miss most your saying 'hi' to me." She smiled
as broadly as the ocean—namesake for her store—and said
"Have a great evening!" As if, despite my age and disability, I were
going to a party now, one where she would sit and talk to me
as I used to talk to girlfriends, curled up on a settee, telling
the deepest secrets about everything and nothing, and all for the sake
of a musky scent hanging over the place we happened on
by accident, just by being a certain age in a century soon to be forgotten.

Jade Ware

Herbal Emancipation

Unable to ignore the comfort factor
I have seen chronic illnesses soothed
Some clamor for the almighty medicinal card
Only to partake during videogame intermissions
Enter the great debate although I don't comprehend the reason
It grows from the earth but capitalism demands systematic
Regulation for the love of money
Relaxation, taxation it should be free
If you ask me but who am I?
Just someone living in the home of the brave
For certainly this is not the land of the *truly* free
Marijuana caused such Reefer Madness in black and white
In its purest form it is good, simply good
Recreationally or as an herb
It is good and if only we could think past
The almighty dollar, we would realize
It was here long before we argued over it and
Long before cardholders were allowed
Medicinal proportions
Emancipate the herb
Our nation is far too stressed and uptight
Prozac is winning the race - Pick up the pace Cannabis!
You can do this, we need you to ease these troubled minds, bodies and souls

Richard Bannerman

The Wrapped Lace

Jase lit the joint with his decorated Zippo lighter and took a puff. He then released it as he leaned against the wall. He didn't want to faint and he definitely didn't want to drop the joint. His nerves were bad enough without his parents interfering and causing a mess again. He then heard a knock on his bedroom door.

Jase muttered "Shit..." as he hurried to put away the joint.

His older brother, Humberto, opened the door as he said "Hey, champ, what are you up...to...?" and saw Jase with the joint.

Jase sighed and answered "Making sure that I don't struggle tomorrow. Ridgedale only had 900 kids. How am I going to deal in a huge place like Portmount?"

Humberto replied "You keep calm and handle your nerves...sorry."

Jase snorted and said "That's part of why I'm taking this stuff, remember? To stop whatever's making me shake and kick off like this. It's better than having to go through medical treatments anyway."

Humberto asked "How are you getting this stuff? I mean, how do you know if it's safe?"

Jase answered "I got it from a friend and I know it's safe because I trust him and he hasn't let me down as of yet. Mom and Dad won't get a prescription from a doctor.

We're poor so I guess it doesn't matter. That's also part of why they sent me to Portmount."

Humberto frowned and responded with "I thought they made you transfer because you were having trouble at Ridgedale."

Jase replied "That was it. I was shaking, having trouble keeping myself still. Some of the other kids started calling me "Twitchy". So I started cutting classes and hanging out downtown, you know, at the movie theaters and at the mall. Mom and Dad got angry and said that if I got expelled, they'd send me to military school."

Jase continued "I heard about weed from a kid at school so I did some research and found out it could help calm tremors. I got some from a friend and Dad caught me using one afternoon when he came home early. He hit me and took it away. That's when he and Mom decided to send me to Portmount. It's my punishment since there aren't any military schools that are local."

Humberto asked "How much have you been taking?"

Jase answered "Not a lot. I usually take a couple pinches, roll it into a joint and smoke it in the mornings or afternoons."

Humberto said "I've heard that it can mess you up, though. I mean, physically. Are you sure that you should be taking as much as you are?"

Jase shrugged and responded with "I haven't had any problems so far. As long as I'm subtle and I keep the air in the room clean, Mom and Dad won't know a thing."

Humberto sighed and said "I hope you know what you're doing. I'm glad weed's helping you but I also think that you might be putting a little too much faith in it."

Jase replied "I'll be just fine. Oh, could you close the door on your way out? I want to air the room out before Dad comes up."

Humberto said "Fine." and closed the door as he left the room. Jase took another puff of the joint as he moved and sat on his bed. He then opened the window and began to swipe his hand around.

Kerry A. Bennett

Medicine Smoke

Inhaling,
I slide into a world
Full of wonder,
Relaxing into my inner space
Of who I want to be.
The seriousness of this life
Slips away
And I dance with my inner spirit
Round the fire in my mind,
Stepping to the beat of primal drums
That urge me to remember
Who I am,
Who I was,
And who I am becoming.

Ego falls away
As I spin perfect circles
Around my soul,
Letting go
Of material perceptions
That hold me bound
In the mundane world.

Deeper I float
Through the smoke
And into the fire
Where I become reborn,
Rising into the night sky,
Reunited with those that came before.

I feel my roots,
Pulling me back
Into myself

And I smile in simple joy,
Finding my inner peace
Welcoming me
Like a long lost friend,
Home again.

Kristin Roedell

Dirty Girl

Fall and winter mornings
were awash with mist.
It took me an hour
to circle the lake;
I sat on every bench,
I memorized the plaques.

A moss-covered tree stretched
branches across the shallows;
the ducks were pearled along
them, waiting for the winter sun
to come up,
bills tucked into feathers.

I saw God
in the simple angles
that followed them
as they swam.
When startled, they lifted
in a flood of wings, returning
like a gentle rain.

September
I sat under a red and gold oak,
leaves spread beneath me
in a rich gown.
December
I walked the high trails,
a hoarfrost on the reeds.
I wrote a poem (this poem)

to not forget the sound
of leaves underfoot.

I have never known
such a graceful falling
of the year.

It might have been
the marijuana,
pungent and strong;
I smoked it that year.
They called it
Dirty Girl—

but I have never been
so clean.

Christopher Luna

We're Goin' to Sev (c. 1995)

my suburban heart belongs to 7Eleven
a place
to wander
around in
    high
        suffering from
        the munchies
unable to make a fucking decision

        eye housewives
    in torn sweats and flip flops
bent over ice cream freezers

    and wonder
    what is to
    become of me

Sev: a liminal space
that manifests itself
in front of a house
anywhere in Nassau County, Strong Island
turns out Dr. Leary was right on
    concerning set and setting
'cause there's nowhere I'd rather be
than sitting in this car with my family
sharing this sacred plant in safety
this moment
perfectly—
cough
bow
and pass
that sucker around

Nathan Tompkins

A Joint Circle

We sit in a circle on Waterfront Park,
the slight summer wind bouncing
off the Willamette River, as two hits
of acid melt from the paper on my tongue.

Take a deep hit off the bong,
listen to the water bubble
as the smoke goes up the stem
past the lips, down the windpipe
to briefly settle in the lungs,
before being forced out
the burning throat with torrential coughs.

Roll a joint between four fingers,
lick, light, pass it as we rise, smoke,
feel the bongos pulsate in time
with the beat of our hearts,

tramp the bare feet in ground,
pushing the grass blades beneath
the surface of the sweat mud,

Then we sit back down, three joints
circling six people, as we continue
our late night flight over the river.

Tiffany Burba-Schramm

New York High

We walked the light paved streets,
high from the energy of the city;
high from the weed that my brother
gave us as a welcome to New York gift.

The sounds pulse ever so deeply
within our scattered minds,
Time Square is like Vegas on depressants,
but still bright and over stimulating.

Sight after sight; sound after sound we keep the beat,
dance in the streets under a water fall of lights,
smile at strangers; drink with poets and comedians.

At the end of the night we settle in by smoking more.
Write the corpse poems about aging bones
and how the stairs seem most difficult.

Morning is orange sunlight on sober faces.
The heat of the Fall sun gives me a slight tan.
I wake him as I carry the wooden box to sit beside his bed.

"Wake and bake," he states through his groggy dry lips.
I just smile and say, "I can't think of a better day."

Tiffany Burba-Schramm

Getting High

Pop can
Pipe
bong
blunt
It's all a different high
smoke it
eat it
have your lover blow smoke into your mouth, end it with a kiss
It's all about the high
paranoid
super chill
write the poetry
sing the song
It's all the effects of the high
lost in time
float through the sky
connect deep to the person on the inside
It's really just about getting by
Lost inhibitions
put down ammunition
Visine hides red eyes
It's all about getting high.

Scott Thomas Outlar

Priming the Pump for a Fire

Different strands of cannabis
affect consciousness
with subtle shifts
in varied directions.
This current one
has slowed down the fire
in my neurons
to the point
where I'm using sheer will
to fan the flames
down near the embers
so the ink can flow once more.
I will win.
The flames will never die completely.
The pen will never go empty.
The Phoenix is always
waiting in the wings,
ready to rise,
ready to soar,
ready to rain down from above
with a love so pure it hurts,
with a hatred so clean it lasts forever,
with a flare for the truth,
with an apocalyptic fervor,
with a Renaissance,
with a Revolution around the sun,
with a Revelation
from somewhere deep –
that eternal fountain,
that wellspring,
that nectar of the gods
which never runs dry.

Tim Kahl

The Devil's Lettuce

You smoke it and I put a sprig in my tea.
You grind the seeds for a wonderful cupcake topping.
I drop it in my eyes so that I can clearly see
the trampled vintage where
the grapes of wrath are stored.
We mellow as though devoted to a squad
of little yellow pills that keep the heart ship shape.
For afterwards, Doritos are the antidote to
the pangs of munchimania that conspire
to keep us happy-go-fucky in this lovely landscape.
Oh my little giggle nuggets.
Oh my left-handed cigarette.
Grant us holy insight into
the science of your charms
and how indubitably you improve the mood.
Yes, I'm sure our sheer joy is highly taxable,
and this pure euphoria is just a rental,
but who am I to tell you how you should own
the time you spend in a chair.
Let us take our place in
the great garganjuan tentacle
and let's forgive this plot hatched by
our computers to keep us calm and stupid
so they can take over every bit of thinking
and acting — once and for all.

Erev Rosh Hashanah 5773

Yemaya in my ears
Marijuana through me,
        threw me
    true me?

This is a woman's body
A woman alive in her senses.
Beside, beneath, beyond the pain,
the heat, the chocolate melt.

Mercedes Webb-Pullman

When You Run Out of Papers, There's Always the Gideon

I roll another holy smoke
and burn to ash the word of God.
I reach Nirvana in one toke;
I roll another. Holy Smoke!
These North Coast buds can make you choke.
I'll swear they're strong as Jacob's rod!
I roll another holy smoke
and burn to ash. The word of God.

Bill Gainer

Living Easy

> Gave up the booze,
> just smoke dope
> anymore.
> I like the stuff
> the Mexicans grow.
> It takes you places,
> heaven
> sometimes.
> The doctor
> wrote a prescription,
> said it's a good thing
> to have
> when you're medicating
> with angels.

High Above The Pain

Today, I will claim to have the pot flu
on herbal medication
sitting on my back porch
watching a blackbird
casually jump from one branch to another.

I take another toke
as deep bone arthritic pain subsides.
Able to move about normally,
I get up and walk out
to stand under the elm tree
to get a closer look at his ballet.

The blackbird, pissed off
at my intrusion, screeches down at me,
zig-zagging gracefully
to higher branches to get away from
this rude, old man, smiling up at it,
who is finally high above the pain.

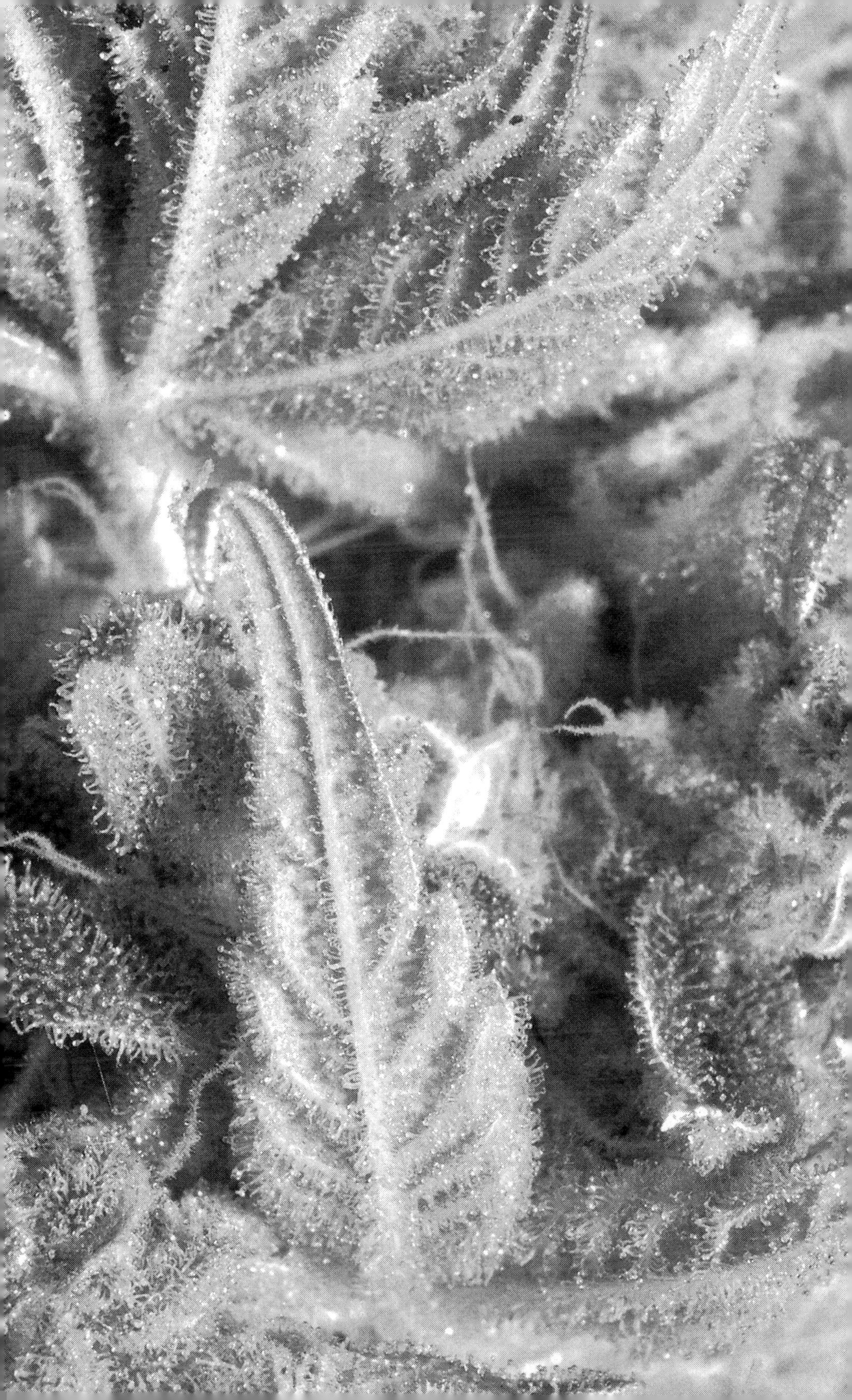

Acknowledgments

We gratefully acknowledge the following publications in which these poems and stories first appeared:

"Flowers" appeared in S. K. Kelen's book, *Earthly Delights* (Pandanus Books, Canberra, 2006).

"Toucans & Reindeer" by Chella Courington was first published in *riverrabble 17* (Summer Bloomsday Issue, 2010).

"Tokus" by Cathy Bryant first appeared online at http://www.englishpen.org/outreach/read-todays-made-up-word-22.

A version of "Ivy and Weed" (as "Cancer Beetles") by Shawn Aveningo was first published in *Boston Poetry,* 2014.

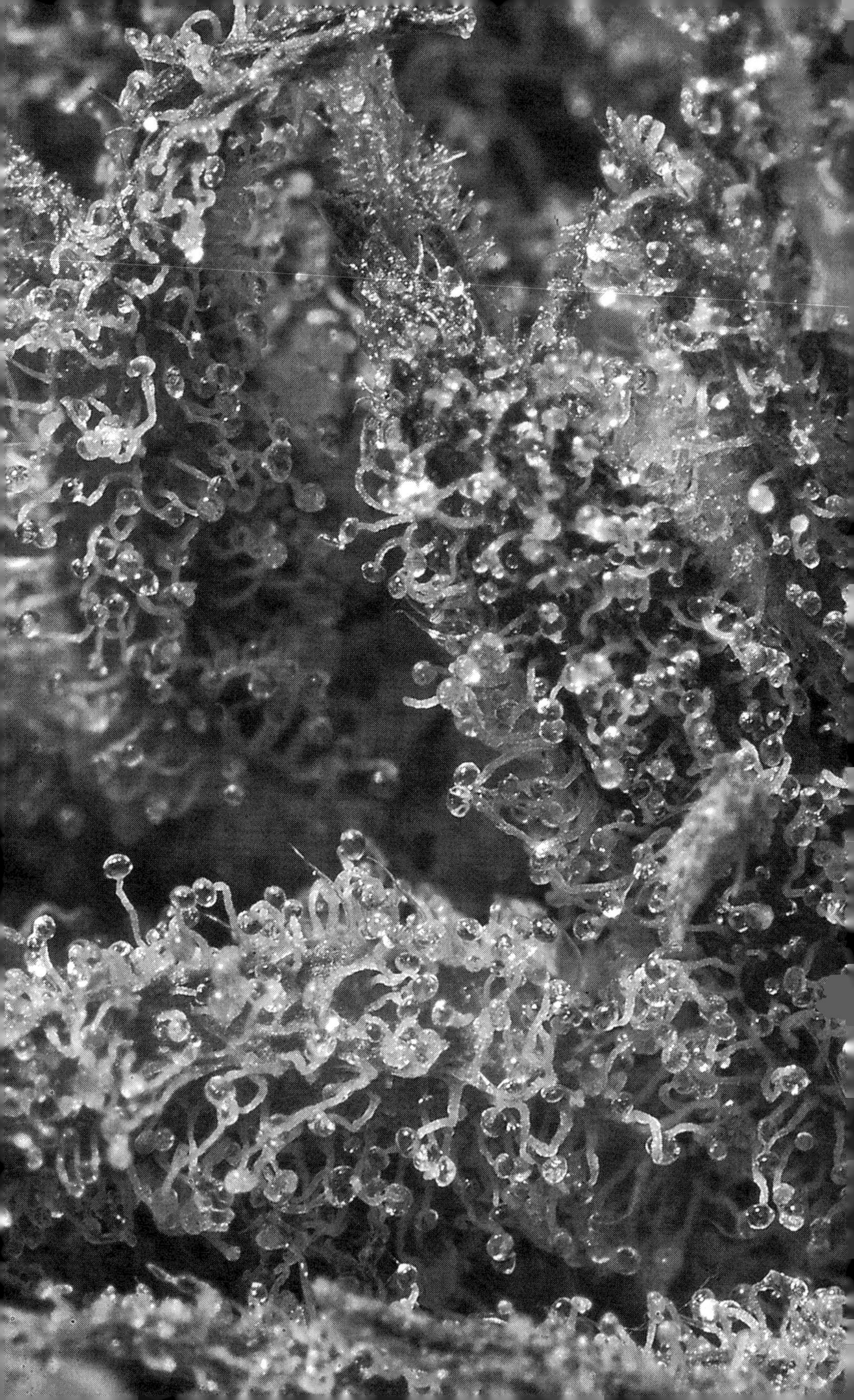

Contributors

Adrian Ernesto Cepeda is an LA Poet who is currently enrolled in the MFA Graduate program at Antioch University where he lives with his wife and their cat Woody Gold. His poetry is featured in *The Yellow Chair Review*, *Silver Birch Press* and was *Cultured Vultures'* Top 3 Poems of the Week. <adrianernestocepeda.com>

Alec Solomita's first short story, written when he was 13, was about senility; that is his character note. Since then, he's published fiction and poetry in *The Mississippi Review*, *Southwest Review*, and *MadHatLit*, among others. Although he is not an employee, he is disgruntled. He does not live in Brooklyn. <solomitaalec@gmail.com>

Angi Holden is a freelance writer, whose work includes adult & children's poetry, short stories & flash fictions. Doobie honest, she can live without cannabis, but not without writing.

Poet, deep ecologist. and Rainbow Family elder, **Art Goodtimes** of Norwood weaves baskets, grows potatoes and is Colorado's only Green Party county commissioner. Founder of Talking Gourds poetry events since 1989. Poet Laureate of the Western Slope (2011-13). Most recent book *Looking South to Lone Cone* (Western Eye Press, 2013) <talkinggourds.weebly.com>

Barbara Ruth is interested in curlicues of the mind and finding words for what is unutterable, and then resting in the places without words. She does these things in San Jose, California where she also writes memoir, fiction, essays, as well as poems. She is also a published photographer.

Bill Gainer is internationally known as a writer, editor, promoter, humorist and poet. He is the publisher of the PEN Award winning R. L. Crow Publications and is the ongoing host of Red Alice's Poetry Emporium. Gainer is widely published and recognized across the country for giving legendary fun filled performances. His latest book, *Lipstick and Bullet Holes*, is from Epic Rites Press, Canada (2014). <billgainer.com>

Brad G. Garber lives, writes and runs around naked in the Great Northwest. He fills his home with art, music, photography, plants, rocks, bones, books, good cookin' and love. He has published poetry, essays and articles in many quality publications. 2013 Pushcart Prize nominee. <bggarber@yahoo.com>

Brandyn Johnson is an adjunct English instructor for Black Hills State University. His poetry has appeared in *Sugar House Review*, *Dunes Review*, and *The American Aesthetic* among others. His daughter, Ari was born on the Ides of March by way of Caesarian section. <brandyn.johnson@bhsu.edu>

Burky Achilles began a spontaneous eruption of poetry in January of 2014. Her poetry was selected as the 2015 first-place winner in the Tucson Festival of Books Literary Awards. Upcoming 2016 publications include prose pieces in *Fifty Over Fifty* an anthology by Rosemont College and *VoiceCatcher*. <burkyachilles@gmail.com>

Carl "Papa" Palmer, retired Army, retired FAA, now just plain retired, lives in University Place, WA. He has seven chapbooks and a contest winning poem riding a bus somewhere in Seattle. Motto: Long Weekends Forever.

Freelance writer **Carolyn Smuts** taught history before fleeing academic life to write fiction. Her most recent works were published by Akashic Books, Omnific, and Jitter Press. She lives in Southern California and has an admittedly pathetic need for 'likes' on her Facebook page, Written and Rewritten. <writtenandrewritten@hotmail.com>

Casey Bush has been a Portland poet since the 1970s and published seven books of verse including *The Blessings of Madness* (1994) and *Kiss of the Apocalypse* (2002). He is a Senior Editor of *The Bear Deluxe Magazine* which explores environmental issues through the literary and graphic arts.

Catfish McDaris won the Thelonius Monk Award in 2015. His 25 years of published material is in the Special Archives Collection at Marquette University in Milwaukee, Wisconsin. His ancestors are from the Aniwaya Clan of the Cherokee Nation. <Mcdar3@aol.com>

Cathy Bryant has won 22 literary awards, and can't quite believe it. Her published books are: *Contains Strong Language and Scenes of a Sexual Nature*, *Look at All the Women*, *How to Win Writing Competitions (and make money)* and *Pride & Regicide*. See Cathy's listings for cash-strapped writers at compsandcalls.com. <www.cathybryant.co.uk>

When not hiking and chasing after cats, **Chella Courington** writes, reads, and teaches. Her recent novella, *The Somewhat Sad Tale of the Pitcher and the Crow*, is available at Amazon. Reared in the Appalachian South, she now lives in

California but can still buck dance fifteen minutes straight. <chellacourington@gmail.com>

Clark County, WA Poet Laureate **Christopher Luna** is the co-founder, with Toni Partington, of Printed Matter Vancouver, which has published two volumes of poems from Ghost Town Poetry Open Mic, the popular Vancouver, WA reading he founded in 2004. Recent publications include *Gobshite Quarterly* and *Bombay Gin*. <www.printedmattervancouver.com>

D. Russel Micnhimer has been writing poetry for forty five years while working at a variety of jobs and traveling through much of the world pursuing his interests in the archaeology of ancient civilizations and rock art. <talkingearth@hotmail.com>

David Belmont is working on his first novel and a memoir. An indie musician before the phrase was coined, he has produced over 30 albums since 1975. Past work includes collaborations with poet Jose Angel Figueroa (including Transfigurations, Public Theatre, 1976). He is currently co-music director of the Castillo Theatre, NYC. <davidbelmont.com>

Devin Taylor studies English and Creative-Writing at Washington College in Chestertown. He reads poetry at open mics all over the Washington DC area, sometimes under the pseudonym 'Chuck E. Cheese.' He has forthcoming publications in *Gargoyle* magazine and the inaugural issue of *Silicon Heart Zine*. He plays electric kazoo. <devinbt@gmail.com>

Doug Draime's latest book is *More Than The Alley*, a poetry collection from Interior Noise Press. Short story writer, and playwright, Draime emerged as a presence in the literary 'underground' in Los Angeles. Forthcoming, *Farrago Soup*, career spanning opus from Pedestrain Press. He has smoked pot with the best.

Eileen Malone's poetry has been published in over 500 literary journals and anthologies earning three Pushcart nominations. Her collection *Letters with Taloned Claws* was published by Poets Corner Press (Sacramento) and her book *I Should Have Given Them Water* was published by Ragged Sky Press (Princeton). <eileenmalone@us.com>

Eric Silvera's writing has appeared in *Nerve*, Vol. 1 Brooklyn, and *Underground Voices*, won *Slice Magazine*'s 'Bridging the Gap' prize, and was shortlisted for

Matrix Magazine's 2010 Lit POP award. He received his MFA from the City College of New York and can't resist himself when walking past Taco Bell. <eric.silvera@gmail.com>

Halee Kirkwood is a recent graduate of Northland College, with a degree in creative writing and gender studies. When not babysitting books at a local bookstore or the public library, Kirkwood finds time to edit *Aqueous Magazine*, a Lake Superior-based literature & visual arts publication. <halee.kirkwood@gmail.com>

Helen Sparrow is an unabashed tea snob and incorrigible night owl. She has previously placed in multiple writing contests in her hometown of Dayton, Ohio. <hdsparrow@ymail.com>

Jade Ware is a freelance writer and published poet having contributed to several anthologies and online publications including *BlazeVox, Vox Poetica* and *Clean Sheets*. Jade was a radio personality on KFAT in Anchorage. Phoenix is now her home where she resides with her beautiful daughter Mercedes-Nicole. Poetry is her passion. <ware329@yahoo.com>

Jake Grieco is a 23-year-old MFA candidate at the Jack Kerouac School of Disembodied Poetics at Naropa University. His work has appeared in *BlazeVOX, Aberration Labyrinth, Mad Swirl*. He currently serves as Senior Editor of *Bombay Gin* the literary journal of the Kerouac School.

Jane James has a terror of writing bios. Put in interviewing Terry Wogan on live TV? Leave out becoming an accidental greengrocer? She has performed poetry at a cacophony of festivals and slams and had poems published in anthologies *The Mortal Man* and *Earthwords*. She is quite old. Is that it? <jane.j@operamail.com>

Jayne Martin's work appears in *Boston Literary Magazine, Midwestern Gothic,* and *Literary Orphans*. Her book, *Suitable for Giving; A Collection of Wit with a Side of Wry*, made a reader snort a coffee out his nose. She lives on a mountaintop in California where no Jehovah's Witness can find her. <injaynesworld.blogspot.com>

Jennifer Pratt-Walter loves simple yet magnificent reasons to write poetry. Her publishings include *VoiceCatcher, Sage Woman, Poetry in the Shops, Spirited Women*, and currently, *Poetry Moves*, a Clark-county wide rolling poetry show in the C-Tran buses.

Jill Hawkins is a recent graduate student of the Red Earth MFA program at Oklahoma City University. Jill has publications of poems: "No Reservations" in *Southwestern American Literature*, Spring 2016, and "Thoracic Park" in The *Journal the American Medical Association* (JAMA), Summer 2015. <jillbrady73@yahoo.com>

Jim Fulcomer is an octogenarian poet who lives in Lincoln CA. He self-publishes as an amusement and hobby, hoping for a wider audience who appreciates the nearly-lost art of rhyming poetry. <jjfulcomer@mac.com>

John Lambremont, Sr. is a poet from Baton Rouge, Louisiana. His recent published works include *Dispelling The Indigo Dream*, Local Gems Poetry Press, 2013, and *What It Means To Be A Man (And Other Poems Of Life And Death)*, Finishing Line Press, 2014. <bigriverpoetry.com>

John Smistad is a multi-published and sometimes awarded writer of short stories, movie reviews, essays and poetry. May you get off on his half-baked tale, "Trippin". It may not be high art, but it just might sneak up on ya out of the weeds. <thequickflickcritic.blogspot.com>

Judith Skillman's latest collection is *House of Burnt Offerings* from Pleasure Boat Studio. She tried medical marijuana in August, 2014. She drove to Olive Street, got lost, then waited for two hours to speak to the doctor and learned very little. Her poems appear in *Tampa Review*, *Cimarron Review*, *Poetry*, and elsewhere. <judith.skillman@comcast.net>

Karen Jane Cannon's poems have appeared in a variety of journals and anthologies. She was commended for The Flambard Poetry Prize 2014. <karen-jane-cannon.co.uk>

Karen Robiscoe's work has appeared in numerous literary journals including: *Spectrum* at UCSB, *Lunch Ticket* at Antioch, Los Angeles, *Steamticket*, *Dark Light 3*, *Main Street Rag*, *Meat for Tea*, *Sand Canyon Review*, *Blue Crow*, *Midnight Circus*, and *300 Days of Sun*. Fowlpox Press released her chapbook: *Word Mosaics* in 2014. <charronschatter.com>

A nine-time Pushcart-Prize nominee and National Park Artist-in-Residence, **Karla Linn Merrifield** has eleven books to her credit, the newest of which is *Bunchberries, More Poems of Canada*, a sequel to. *Godwit: Poems of Canada* (FootHills Publishing). She is editor/poetry book reviewer for *The Centrifugal Eye*. <karlalinn.blogspot.com.>

Katy Brown, retired Social Worker, poet, and photographer, whose work appears online and in numerous journals and anthologies has won a ton of impressive awards in various competitions; and has been nominated for the Pushcart Prize. Her secret power is that she can catch a lizard with a blade of grass. <kbrown4081@aol.com>

Kerry A. Bennett is an anthropologist, an environmentalist, a freelance artist, and a writer. She hopes her work will contribute to the paradigm shift that will create a better world.

Kristin Roedell is a Northwest poet and author of *Girls with Gardenias*, (Flutter Press, 2013) and *Downriver* (Aldrich Press 2015). Her works appeared in *Switched on Gutenberg*, The *Journal of the American Medical Association*, and *Crab Creek Review*. She lives with a menagerie of ferrets, collies, cats, and one husband.

Leah Mueller is an independent writer from Tacoma, Washington. She is the author of two full-length books, *Allergic to Everything* (Writing Knights Press, 2015) and *The Underside of the Snake* (Red Ferret Press, 2015). Her work has appeared in *Origins Journal, Talking Soup, Silver Birch Press*, and many others. <wackypoetlady.blogspot.com>

Leona Phillips is a leprechaun, a ferret, a moonbeam, a tree. She lives and grows and bursts into flames and emerges again from a pile of glitter in a land where all the animals walk on stilts. She writes other things under other names and often eats too much peppermint.

LOB has been a creative force for over 25 years as Thee Instagon Foundation, publishing poetry, music, art, plus managing and organizing events. He believes in the creative potential in all people. He smokes weed every day. <tif.org>

Lori Loranger's poems have appeared in *Ghost Town Poetry* anthologies, *Visions of Light*, and *The Poeming Pigeon*. She is a native Washingtonian and longtime resident of the Columbia River Gorge, where she lives with her glassblowing husband, teenage son, a goat and two cats. <lorangerlori@gmail.com>

Lydia Flores is a photographer, poet and lover of light. New York City Native and MFA student at Long Island University. She has work published in *Rain Party & Disaster Society*, *Atlantis* and *Coraddi Magazine*. <inlightofmysoul.tumblr.com>

Marilyn Stablein's books include *Sleeping in Caves: A Sixties Himalayan Memoir* and *Splitting Hard Ground* which won the New Mexico Book Award. She teaches workshops in Memoir and Artist Books. Her work is widely published and she exhibits her collage and artist books internationally. <marilynstablein.com>

Marj Hahne is a freelance editor and writing teacher, a 2015 MFA graduate from the Rainier Writing Workshop, and the founder-director of The Avocado Sisterhood, a membership organization for women and girl writers. <www.MarjHahne.com>

Mercedes Webb-Pullman: IIML Victoria University Wellington New Zealand MA in Creative Writing 2011. Published in: *Turbine, Reconfigurations, The Electronic Bridge*. Proud member of Aotearoa Legalize Cannabis Party.

Michael Berton has had poems appear recently in *Fourteen Hills, Axolotl* and *The 2016 Texas Poetry Calendar*. His second collection of poetry, *No Shade In Aztlan* came out in late 2015. He participated in a Pop-Up reading at the 2015 Wordstock Festival in Portland, Oregon.

Nathan Tompkins is a writer living in Portland, Oregon, though his heart loves dipping its toes in the Kootenai River. His work has appeared in many publications including *Yellow Chair Review* and *Crab Fat Magazine*. He is the author of four chapbooks including *Lullabies to a Whiskey Bottle*. <www.facebook.com/NathanTompkinspoetry>

Paco Marquez's work has appeared in *Apogee, LiVE MAG!*, and is forthcoming in *Ostrich Review* and *Huizache*. He was featured 'Lo-Writer of the Week' in Juan Felipe Herrera's California Poet Laureate website, and on Columbia University WKCR 89.9 FM 'Studio A.' He holds an MFA in poetry from NYU. <pacopoet@gmail.com>

Pattie Palmer-Baker is artist and poet who combines these two forms of expression in collages of paste paper and calligraphy. Because so many viewers respond more strongly to the words rather than the image, she now focuses on writing. <www.pattiepalmerbaker.com>

Peter D. Goodwin divides his time between the streets and vibrant clutter of

NYC and the remnants of the natural world along Maryland's Chesapeake Bay, discovering in the dislocation of environments the creative edge where words rekindle their spark.

Phoebe Levija is a writer living in Washington, DC. She is a first place winner of the Karen Pelz poetry award and has been published in the literary magazine, *Thread*. She spends most of her time contemplating time travel and considering which words sound better in French than English. <womanofculture.com>

Rachael Clyne lives in Glastonbury, UK. Her collection, *Singing at the Bone Tree*, won Indigo Dreams' George Stevens Memorial Prize. Anthologies: *The Very Best of 52*, *Book of Love and Loss*, *Poems for a Liminal Age*. Magazines: *Poetry Space*, *Reach*, *Domestic Cherry*, *Tears in the Fence*. <www.rachaelclyne.com>

Rebecca Bilkau's first poem was published when she was young enough to have her pocket money stopped because her ma thought it was based on experience. *Sending for New Omens* published by Wayleave press in 2015 so far hasn't received such harsh treatment, though it was. <beautiful-dragons.com>

Richard Bannerman is a shy, quiet stranger living in the Northeast who sleeps in the day and wanders during the night. He has a pet to keep him company when he's bored and this is his first publication. <rbcomet6@gmail.com>

S. K. Kelen lives in Australia's bush capital and enjoys hanging around the house, philosophically, and travelling. His most recent books of poems are *Goddess of Mercy*, *Earthly Delights* and *Island Earth: New and Selected Poems*.

Sarah White has been a teacher, a translator, and an Itinerant painter of kitchen doors. Her recent poetry collections are *The Unknowing Muse* (Dos Madres, 2014), *Wars Don't Happen Anymore* (Deerbrook Editions, 2015), and *Alice Ages and Ages* (BlazeVox, 2010), which tells the same story in 50 different styles. <www.sarahwhitepages.com>

Scott Thomas Outlar hosts the site 17Numa.wordpress.com where links to his published work can be found. His words appeared in more than 140 publications in 2015, including *Yellow Chair Review*, *Words Surfacing*, *The First Line*, and *Harbinger Asylum*. Scott's chapbook *Songs of a Dissident* was published through Transcendent Zero Press.

Shawn Avenigno is a globally published poet whose work has appeared in over

80 literary journals and anthologies. She's a Pushcart nominee, co-founder of The Poetry Box® and journal designer for *VoiceCatcher*. Shawn is a proud mother of three and shares the creative life publishing books and websites with her husband in Beaverton, Oregon. <www.redshoepoet.com>

Sigrun Susan Lane is a Seattle poet. Her poems have appeared in regional and national publications, including *Malahat Review*, *Seattle Review* and *Sing Heavenly Muse*. She is the author of a chapbook, *Little Bones*, published in 2013. She delights in seeing the progressive changes to drug policies across our country.

SM, of Roseville, CA is not really a fan or opponent of Cannabis, but prefers the penname because it sounds like a fun thing to do, like saying, "I'm Batman." Check out *Dad's Desk*, *Brevities*, and *Ina Coolbrith Gathering 13* for some poetry favorites.

Having failed as a bronc rider—the rodeo circuit not being a good fit—**Spurs Broken** sought out a higher calling: Dragon slaying. Unfortunately, that too was a bust so he mastered baiting hooks down at the local pier. Fishing was good, but photography was better; he wisely opted for a career in the graphic and visual communication arts, where he won a bunch of awards. He's quite proud of his two adult children. Both are artists as well, except one thinks she's also a dragon slayer. <spursbroken.com>

Teresa Zemaitis teaches Creative Writing and Journalism at the high school level. She is only a few credits away from finishing her MFA. Her addictions to coffee and her dogs get her through the days, as does the support of her husband of 25 years. <zemaitist@hotmail.com>

Tiffany Burba-Schramm is a poet and a photographer that lives in Vancouver Washington. Tiffany has been published with a project called *Poets in the Shops*, *Ghost Town Anthology* Volume 2, and most recently was published for the project *Poetry Moves* where her poem will appear on C-Tran buses. <tiffanyburbaschrammcom.wordpress.com>

Tim Kahl has always been fascinated with the intricacies of stoner etiquette though he fails miserably at trying to conform to it. He is a master of the errant comment and the vacant stare. Under the influence, he has uttered the longest sentence of his adult life, but he is rendered completely incapable of speaking German after he finds the carb. <www.timkahl.com>

Tricia Knoll is a straight-arrow poet who veers left at any opportunity. Her chapbook *Urban Wild* (Finishing Line Press, 2014) examines how human and wildlife interact in urban habitat. *Ocean's Laughter* (Aldrich Press, 2016) combines lyric and eco-poetry, love poems for the northern Oregon coast, specifically Manzanita. <triciaknoll.com>

Wayne Lee used to write all his poetry while high, which is one reason most of those poems sucked. <wayneleepoet.com>

William Doreski is a fun and interesting guy who hasn't smoked dope in years but generally approves of it. His work has appeared here and there. <williamdoreski.blogspot.com>

Index of Authors

The following authors whose work(s) begin on the annotated page number(s) are indexed by last name:

Achilles, Burky: 96
Aveningo, Shawn: 112
Bannerman, Richard: 121
Belmont, David: 87
Bennett, Kerry A.: 35, 123
Berton, Michael: 25
Bilkau, Rebecca: 55
Broken, Spurs: 68
Brown, Katy: 61, 65
Bryant, Cathy: 72
Burba-Schramm, Tiffany: 129, 130
Bush, Casey: 78
Cannon, Karen Jane: 32
Cepeda, Adrian Ernesto: 52, 91
Clyne, Rachael: 94
Courington, Chella: 71
Doreski, William: 44
Draime, Doug: 33, 136
Flores, Lydia: 73
Fulcomer, Jim: 39
Gainer, Bill: 86, 135
Garber, Brad G.: 62
Goodtimes, Art: 118
Goodwin, Peter D.: 42
Grieco, Jake: 17, 100
Hahne, Marj: 99
Hawkins, Jill: 106
Holden, Angi: 15, 60
James, Jane: 38
Johnson, Brandyn: 48
Kahl, Tim: 34, 132
Kelen, S.K.: 22

Kirkwood, Halee: 98
Knoll, Tricia: 54
Lambremont, John, Sr.: 114
Lane, Sigrun Susan: 18
Lee, Wayne: 40
Levija, Phoebe: 19
LOB: 66
Loranger, Lori: 28
Luna, Christopher: 50, 127
Malone, Eileen: 57
Marquez, Paco: 16
Martin, Jayne: 36
McDaris, Catfish: 29
Merrifield, Karla Linn: 77
Micnhimer, D. Russel: 90
Mueller, Leah: 110
Outlar, Scott Thomas: 131
Palmer, Carl "Papa": 41
Palmer-Baker, Pattie: 76
Phillips, Leona: 70
Pratt-Walter, Jennifer: 51
Robiscoe, Karen: 47, 116
Roedell, Kristin: 125
Ruth, Barbara: 133
Silvera, Eric: 30
Skillman, Judith: 21, 119
SM: 27
Smistad, John: 82
Smuts, Carolyn: 53
Solomita, Alec: 92
Sparrow, Helen: 107
Stablein, Marilyn: 109
Taylor, Devin: 93
Tompkins, Nathan: 80, 128
Ware, Jade: 59, 120
Webb-Pullman, Mercedes: 134
White, Sarah: 105
Zemaitis, Teresa: 102

About The Poetry Box®

The Poetry Box® was founded in 2011 by Shawn Aveningo & Robert R. Sanders, who whole-heartedly believe that every day spent with the people you love, doing what you love, is a moment in life worth celebrating. It all started out as our way to help people memorialize the special milestones in their lives by melding custom poems with photographic artwork for anniversaries, birthdays, holidays and other special occasions. Robert and Shawn expanded on their shared passion for creating poetry and art with the introduction of The Poetry Box® Book Publishing.

The book you now hold in your hands, *The Poeming Pigeon — A Literary Journal of Poetry,* evolved from the first issue (*Poeming Pigeons: Poems about Birds*) Each semi-annual issue will have a unique theme, with Homer, *The Poeming Pigeon* mascot, taking flight to deliver poems to poetry lovers across the globe. Details and submission guidelines can be found at www.ThePoemingPigeon.com.

As Robert and Shawn continue to celebrate the talents of their fellow artisans and writers, they now offer professional book design and publishing services to poets looking to publish their collections of poems.

And as always, The Poetry Box® believes in giving back to the community. Each month a portion of all sales will benefit a different charity. For a complete list of the charities currently supported, please visit the Giving Back page on their website at www.ThePoetryBox.com.

Feel free to visit The Poetry Box® online bookstore, where you'll find more books including:

Keeping It Weird: Poems & Stories of Portland, Oregon

Verse on the Vine: A Celebration of Community, Poetry, Art & Wine

The Way a Woman Knows by Carolyn Martin

Of Course, I'm a Feminist! edited by Ellen Goldberg

Poeming Pigeons: Poems about Birds

The Poeming Pigeon: Poems about Food

and more ...

Order Form

Need more copies for friends and family? No problem. We've got you covered with two convenient ways to order:

1. Go to our website at www.thePoetryBox.com and click on Bookstore.

or

2. Fill out the order form. Email it to Shawn@thePoetryBox.com

---

Name: _____

Shipping Address: _____

_____

Phone Number: (____) _____

Email Address: _____@_____

Payment Method: __Cash __Check __PayPal Invoice __Credit Card

Credit Card #: _____ CCV _____

Expiration Date: _____ Signature: _____

The *Poeming Pigeon — Doobie or Not Doobie?*

# of Copies: _____

x $15.00: _____

Plus Shipping & Handling: _____
($3 per book, or $7.95 for 3 or more books)

Order Total: _____

Thank You!

Made in the USA
San Bernardino, CA
31 March 2016